Pamela,

Every new day,

Bishop Dr. Edward Barnett

Living
Wittingly

Living Wittingly

HIGHER DIMENSION:
From Mercy To Grace and From Grace To Glory

BISHOP EDWARD BARNETT

Author Reputation Press LLC
45 Dan Road Suite 5
Canton MA 02021
www.authorreputationpress.com
Hotline: 1(800) 220-7660
Fax: 1(855) 752-6001

Ordering Information:
Quantity sales. Special discounts are available on quantity purchases by corporations, associations, and others. For details, contact the publisher at the address above.

Printed in the United States of America.

ISBN-13:   Softcover   978-1-64961-483-4
              eBook   978-1-64961-484-1

Library of Congress Control Number: 2021910207

TABLE OF CONTENTS

FOREWORD

By Cain Hope Felder, Professor of Biblical Studies
Howard University School of Divinity

Most of us have heard the expression, "He/she is a witty person," meaning that the individual is capable of spontaneous, clever, often humorous expressions that may also be sarcastic. *Wit* derives from an archaic English word for *knowledge*. In this new evangelical book, *Living Wittingly: From Mercy to Grace, from Grace to Glory,* by Bishop Dr. Edward Barnett, readers will perceive Dr. Barnett's sincere desire to motivate churchgoers to renew their faith. This book also offers the unchurched opportunities to seek out new and powerful biblical teachings. Bishop Dr. Edward Barnet has assembled a collection of his own meditations, capsule sermons, and Bible teachings. This book was written especially for those African Americans who languish on the margins of society and in prisons. There they are increasingly warehoused by our often-reprehensible American criminal justice system.

Dr. Barnett was not born with the proverbial silver spoon in his mouth and was not always comfortable in the church. Discomfort, in fact, humbled him into forswearing false pride and accepting the Christian outreach. That outreach has transformed him into a stable husband, strong father, and multitalented pastor. His story unfolds within these pages as a public record of the difference that God and the unique witness of Jesus of Nazareth can make in one's life! Yet this is not an autobiography as much as an evangelical "pep talk" for those who know their lives have become empty and devoid of meaningful relationships—even devoid of meaning! Here is a nondenominational call from a pastor and bishop for increasingly cynical victims of poverty, isolation, and despair to find their way back to Christian communities. These communities have brushed off their welcome mats and extended their hands, full of mercy and grace, to receive them. The invitations are genuine overtures for more of us to expand the ranks of Christian leaders who can point the way to a higher purpose and stronger cohesion.

The title of this book is inspired by the blessing narrative found in Genesis 48:8–20. In these verses, Jacob (here called Israel) attempts to bless Joseph's two sons. The aged Jacob uses his "wits" and cleverly attempts to bless the younger son, Manasseh. Perhaps mindful of Jacob's theft of his older brother Esau's birthright, Joseph also is witty enough to interrupt the blessing process by guiding Jacob's hand to the elder brother, Ephraim, so that Ephraim is blessed first. Joseph's quick thinking and action helped to insure Ephraim a greater destiny! Readers of this book may also glean a greater sense of God's mercy, grace, and even glory.

Too many of our people do not yet find the church helpful or the teachings of the Bible sufficiently relevant in their lives. Bishop Barnett seeks to inspire his audience and to inform people about the continuing power of faith and the ever-present opportunity to make a fresh start in their personal journeys and negotiate their many challenges.

Bishop Barnett makes the important point that, even today, God wants to bless all those who are vulnerable to victimization. God is still in search of spiritual leaders. That same God is trying to intervene by guiding their hands and hearts to the depths of alienation and pain that so many people suffer here and worldwide. Surely having Barak Obama as the first black president is an astounding precedent. However, it has unleashed a rage that only a bold, divine intervention and interruption will cure. For the sake of real justice, we must address this rage and reduce the high price that the black community has paid for Obama's historic achievement.

PREFACE

And Israel stretched out his right hand, and laid it upon
Ephraim's head, who was the younger, and his left hand upon
Manasseh's head, guiding his hands wittingly; for Manasseh
was the firstborn.

—Genesis 48:14

Do our actions and how we carry them out really make a difference?
Are there strict rules and steps to follow? Can we afford to be oblivious
to the very real consequences of failing to be deliberate in our actions?

Imagine what our lives would be like if we lived each day fully aware
of the Word of God, ever mindful of the meanings and final results of
every action? What if we resolved to adhere to every line and precept?
What if we aimed, with every move and thought, to please God, learn
more about Him, and share His love with others?

On the following pages are my thoughts—many thoughts—as I
considered the possibility of Christians showing, by their actions, that
they actually know what they're doing! Sometimes we don't seem to
be cognizant of the effects of our choices in word and deed. No one
is perfect, but we can determine that we will be and act better. We
do know that each action carries consequences! What we believe, the
level of our trust, the consistency of our worship, the scope of our
understanding, the use of our faith, and how we represent God on
earth matters a great deal. As a pastor, I ponder the optimal ways to

lead, guide, and mentor people; I contemplate what to say, how to say it, and how to demonstrate that Christian life can be lived *consciously*.

There is no better guidance than the Word of God to discover the tools to live wittingly and victoriously.

ACKNOWLEDGMENTS

To my LORD and Savior Jesus Christ who I owe my All I thank you; I love you.

And to my wife of thrity-five years now, Adrienne, the First Lady of Greater Grace Family Ministries Church for thirty years. Thank you so much, baby, for your love, encouragement, and prayers. Little did we know God's plans for us when we met in Pittsburgh twenty-nine years ago. God's ongoing work in our lives is amazing. As we continue to look to God, we purposefully choose to live *in Higher spiritual Dimensions.*

DEDICATION

The second book is dedicated to my wife of 35 years now, my only daughter, and my first grand-baby "Avianna Makai" these three females on different levels have given me everything in life to strive for God's best. His perfect will. I purposefully dedicated myself to God so that I would be granted the wisdom, wealth, and strength to display my Faith openly, unashamed in the power of God. Ladies walk in the virtue passed down to you by your heavenly parent (God) through your faith in Jesus and your nurturing and teaching by the scriptures and the Holy Spirit. Live on that higher dimension with purpose!

I also dedicate this book to all those who seek to live above their natural selves and abilities. God's grace be with you.

It is better to yield to God the higher power above us, so we don't have to fall to things beneath us.

Bishop Dr. Edward Barnett

All to Jesus I surrender. Make me, Savior, wholly Thine. Let me feel the Holy Spirit. Truly know that Thou art mine.

—Judson W. Van DeVenter

Many are the plans in a person's heart, but it is the Lord's purpose that prevails.

—Proverbs 19:21

CHAPTER 1

God's Magnificent Methodology for the Mankind and the World

Then God said, "Let us make mankind in our image, in our likeness, so that they may rule over the fish in the sea and the birds in the sky, over the livestock and all the wild animals, and over all the creatures that move along the ground."

—Genesis 1:26

Lets look at the Love and Mercy God put into existence before creating Humankind. God was methodical and intentional when He created the heavens and the earth. Everything mankind every needed was placed in the earth for man by God but, it only is discovered when it is needed. Even when we don't know the purpose of it or reason for it, God still supplies it because it is necessary at that time. It is great to know that God is NEVER late! He is ALWAYS on time. Everything has a purpose and it all works for the greater purpose of God. Psalms 139 tells us that God knows every thought and movement we make and yet before we were born He put a system in place that we could connect to to bring Him glory. It's hard to believe but He included us from the beginning. His intention was to yield to humanity the care of this unique planet. Imagine the angels—consistent, obedient, and fully aware of God's greatness—marveling at the beauty of nature. Imagine them hoping for a chance to manage the finished works of God's hands. Imagine the seraphim and cherubim, the highest-ranking angels because of their proximity to God, consumed with thoughts of an amazing assignment: to have dominion over the earth.

Made by Him, the heavens are constantly telling of the wonders of God and all His glory. Could you imagine what the angels were singing and saying as God was creating the earth and filling it with crystal, gold, silver, mint, oil, vegetation, and every seed-bearing fruit? Someone had to be given charge over it. Among His creation, who would be assigned to serve as God's ambassadors on the earth?

Imagine the songs of glory celebrating the skill of His hands as He separated the land from the sea and brilliantly created the beasts of the fields from the dust of the ground. Picture the smiles on the angels' faces as He moved through space as if armed with a gigantic paintbrush. Imagine the air as His canvas as He created every flying thing. With the mobility of angels, the birds took to the sky and soared through the firmament. Surely the seraphim and cherubim must have been fascinated by the imagination of God as winged creatures like themselves populated the expanse of the sky.

Can you imagine hearing the voices of the heavens describing the miracle of life breathing in the sea? Who knew that some living creatures could respire in the water, but not in the air? How amazing was it that the Creator would see that the beasts of the field, the fowl of the air, and the animals of the sea would all receive their own specialized environments? Surely the one appointed by God to be His representative on the earth would be the chosen one—God's favorite in the heavens.

How amazing were the works of His hands! Wouldn't it have been reasonable to assume that one of the angels would be assigned to have dominion over the earth? Can you imagine the angels bidding for the assignment? Imagine the disappointment when they learned that He did not find one of them suitable for the assignment. Instead of using something the angels had seen before, God delved within Himself and retrieved another element of His glory. Never before had He done this. He recreated an element of Himself from the dust of the earth and released His natural and supernatural reproductive system of the universe into this creation; one breath was all it took! "Let Us make man in our own image and likeness" It became a living soul when He personally breathed life into it. In His image and likeness, He made humankind a speaking spirit with the ability to engage the world with words and ideas. God spoke into mankind the propensity of fruitfulness (that's productiveness), multiply (that's increase) and dominion(that's ruler-ship over ones life and the ability to keep God's rules).

As the angels engage in their own rather admirable duties, in Psalm 8:1–6, the psalmist David captures the sentiments of the believer.

> Oh Lord, our Lord, how majestic is your name in all the earth! You have set your glory in the heavens. Through the praise of children and infants you have established a stronghold against your enemies, to silence the foe and the avenger. When I consider your heavens, the work of your fingers, the moon and the stars, which you have set in place, what is mankind that you are mindful of them—human beings that you care for them? You have made them a little lower than the angels and crowned them with glory and honor. You made them rulers over the works of your hands; you put everything under their feet.

Who does *that*? Who hands over immeasurable wealth and power without serious thought?

In addition to an incomparable creation for which to care, God gave humankind an exclusive song—a unique declaration. Only we could sing of being blood-washed, redeemed by the blood of the Lamb, delivered from the hands of the enemy, blessed with free will, and granted the opportunity to choose life or death.

CHAPTER 2

Learning Who You Are

I am what God says I am, I can do what God says I can do, I'll have what God says Ill have because He made me and know who I am. When asked to identify yourself, what do you say first? Do you give your name? Is your title more appropriate? Is your job description sufficient? Perhaps, depending on the situation, you identify yourself with a task or an organization, I work here or go to this church. Do you indicate whose son, daughter, spouse, mother, father, or friend you are? Do you think it's necessary to identify yourself? Would you be offended because people should know who you are, based on what you have done or how long you've been on the job? Do you think that there is already enough information out there to identify you? Would anyone be surprised or confused by the way you identify yourself, from what they see?

If you go to places where security checks are required, you must submit some official form of identification, such as a driver's license or a passport. You must have official proof that you are who you say you are. Those photographs had better match your face. If you're asked to give verbally the information on the ID, you should know it by memory to avoid further questions or concerns about your honesty.

Have you ever been confounded at a funeral as speaker after speaker rose to praise the deceased? Perhaps the honoree was meaner than a junkyard dog, yet the eulogists went on and on about how nice he or she was. Have you ever been acquainted with someone for a long time and suddenly realized that you never really knew him or her? How do such different perceptions of identities and characters arise? Do we go out of our way to cover for one another or protect another person's true identity? We may not, but God has certainly tried to do it for each and every one of us. Yet many of us present one identity to some people and a different one to others. Who are we to the people at our jobs or at church? Are we the same people at home? What identity stands out the most: the public one or the private one? Who do you say that you are? Would others be inclined to agree?

Jesus asked His disciples the same question: "Who do men say that I am?" They had a few answers, and only *one* of them answered correctly. Jesus told Peter that there was no way he could have known unless the Holy Ghost revealed it to him. Is God's influence in *us* seen as readily, or does someone else have to point it out?

There's a song entitled, "And They'll Know We Are Christians." It says that the way to identify a Christian is by the *agape* love shown. Is a loving nature the characteristic people associate with us, or are we better known for being divisive, sour, critical, negative, and sarcastic? As we go about our daily lives and engage in what we call "service," is it easy for others to identify us as followers of Christ? Do we spend time reading and studying His words but never truly embracing His way? Are we still thinking that our Christian identity has everything to do with our own actions, attitudes, and accomplishments and little or nothing to do with what God has done by sending Jesus to earth? The undeserved favor or grace of God is at times overwhelming and transforming.

Read Romans 6:8–18 on the dominance of grace in Christian lives.

> Now if we died with Christ, we believe that we will also live with him. For we know that since Christ was raised from the dead, he cannot die again; death no longer has mastery over him. The death he died, he died to sin once for all; but the life he lives—he lives to God. In the same way, count yourselves dead to sin, but alive to God in Christ

Jesus. Therefore, do not let sin reign in your mortal body so that you obey its evil desires. Do not offer any part of yourself to sin as an instrument of wickedness, but rather, offer yourselves to God as those who have been brought from death to life; and offer every part of yourself to him as an instrument of righteousness. For sin shall no longer be your master, because you are not under the law, but under grace. What then? Shall we sin because we are not under the law but under grace? By no means!

The King James translation of the Bible gives Paul's answer: "God forbid!" The passage from Romans continues:

Don't you know that when you offer yourselves to someone as obedient slaves, you are slaves of the one you obey— whether you are slaves to sin (which leads to death) or to obedience (which leads to righteousness)? But, thanks be to God that, though you used to be slaves to sin, you have come to obey, from your heart, the pattern of teaching that has now claimed your allegiance. You have been set free from sin and have become slaves to righteousness.

Notice that the text instructs us to not let sin *reign*. Don't think for one minute that it means that sin is not *present*. Wrongdoing is all too easy, and so is giving in to a sinful nature. We can justify what we do and say all day long, but there is always a penalty for yielding authority to something or someone we *know* shouldn't have it. Experience with sin and its effects should inform us that sin must not be in charge.

Sometimes we make excuses; someone may say, "That's how I was taught," or "I was raised that way." We may often take a stance as if we cannot possibly be wrong, have no capacity to change, or don't intend to change. As Christians, we are always forced to take a closer look at habits, behaviors, and traditions, especially if they don't agree with the Word of God. There are some behaviors and attitudes that we must embrace and others that we must change or even reject if we are going to identify ourselves as new creatures in Christ. We cannot very well say that our way of life is renewed if it is plainly our same old worldview or obviously has our old ways and attitudes all over it.

Second Corinthians 5:17 discusses this kind of renewal. The King James translation reads, "Therefore, if any man be in Christ, he is a new creature: old things are passed away; behold—all things are become new."

Notice those last three words of the text, "are become new." English majors know that *are* is the second person singular and plural of *to be*. It is also the first and third person, plural present indicative, of *to be*. *To be* means "to exist in actuality." *To be* is to have life or reality. How do those two verbs, *are* and *become,* stand comfortably side by side in the same sentence?

According to the dictionary.com an online reference, the word *become* means "to grow or come to be." It means to "change; to undergo a transformation; to enter or assume a certain state or condition." Could it be that this identity in Christ is a past, present, and ongoing condition? Remember that God has always had a plan for us. Relationship with Him was on His mind when He created mankind and sent Jesus into the world. Is there ever a time when I am not striving to appreciate the identity I assumed as a result of the finished work of Christ on Calvary? My identity is then a result of God's transformative work, not my own. It is so important that we not only know who we are, but that we don't make it impossible for others to know whom we serve and represent. The Message Bible translates a portion of 2 Timothy 3:15–16 this way: "There's nothing like the written Word of God for showing you the way to salvation through faith in Christ Jesus. Every part of Scripture is God-breathed and useful one way or another—showing us truth, exposing our rebellion, correcting our mistakes, training us to live God's way."

This identity of ours is not merely an outward one. There's a holiday on the calendar where people dress up and pretend to be someone or something else.

When the holiday is over, people take off those costumes and masks. The pretense is done. The Christian identity, however, cannot be so easily removed, folded up, boxed, and put on a shelf. It is authentic. God has done everything to make it so. There's inner transformation and conviction, not superficial in any way, identifying us as the church—a body of believers.

The Message Bible translates 2 Corinthians 5:17 this way.

> We don't evaluate people by what they have or how they look. We looked at the Messiah that way once, and got it all wrong, as you know. We certainly don't look at him that way anymore. Now we look inside, and what we see is that anyone united with the Messiah, gets a fresh start, is created new. The old life is gone; a new life begins! Look at it! All this comes from the God who settled the relationship between us and him, and then called us to settle our relationships with each other. God put the world square with himself through the Messiah, giving the world a fresh start by offering forgiveness of sins. God has given us the task of telling everyone what he is doing. We're Christ's representatives.
>
> God uses us to persuade men and women to drop their differences and enter into God's work of making things right between them. We're speaking for Christ himself now: Become friends with God; he's already a friend with you.

Our new Christian identity demands that we put away sin and embrace the righteousness that God has so graciously given us.

Read 1 John 1:9 on the power of confession: "If we confess our sins, he is faithful and just and will forgive us our sins and purify us from all unrighteousness."

God so wants to make us new! We have to stop categorizing sin in our own lives and in the lives of others. People like to think that one sin is worse than another. Perhaps it makes them feel more religious or superior in some way. People pick one sin and harp on it. Comparative analysis to determine which sin is worse than another sin is a deceitful and dangerous tactic. Too much time is spent looking down on others for the sins that bind them. That's always easy if the sin in question is something that we don't do. If I don't kill or steal, it's easy to demand that swift justice be meted out to a murderer or a thief. But what about gossip, slander, lying, or sowing seeds of discord? How often do our careless words murder the reputations, careers, relationships, and even the spirits of others? Do we think that a holy God sees any one sin as being worse than another? Wrong is wrong, and sin is sin.

Read 1 John 5:17 for a definition of sin: "All unrighteousness is sin."

It is important for us to see how much we needed Christ's sacrifice. Our identity in Christ is a gift, not a license to attack and harshly judge others according to how upright we think we are. We couldn't earn our new life in Christ, and we certainly didn't deserve it. Why not be thankful, embrace it, and share it?

"But wait a minute," we might say. "What about that slave-and-master thing? I'm not exactly in agreement with that!" It is understandable that most Americans today, especially those of African descent, would have a huge problem with being identified as slaves. We don't want to be any kind of slave, and most of us don't like taking orders! Slavery implies work without pay—unfairness, inequality, and mistreatment. It implies weakness, low self-worth, captivity, and disempowerment. So what is it about this identity in Christ that makes us glad to be slaves of righteousness?

Galatians 4:7 makes a crucial distinction: "So you are no longer a slave but a son, and if you are a son, then you are also an heir through God."

The word *slave*, then, implies a mentality or inclination. That slave mentality we must alter is in our hearts and minds, our perceptions. Trusting God, relying on His strength, and accepting who He says we are and what we have been promised by Him are the mental and emotional changes we must make to move from the slavery mentality to sonship or daughtership. Being crucified with Christ means that the slave mentality, which delights in the flesh, leads to sin, and snubs its nose at consequences, is no longer at the controls. Being heirs of God in these earthly bodies motivates us daily to identify with Christ. If we truly identify with His broken body, His shed blood, His burial, and His resurrection, then we can take heart in developing the strength and discipline to conquer our impulses and temptations to sin! His death was the penalty for the sins of the whole world. A broken world provides an opportunity for us daily to identify with Him.

The apostle Paul specified sin's consequences. Sin results in death. That's how sin pays its willing workers. Fortunately for the believer, sin no longer has a foothold! We are literally joined to Christ. His resurrection signifies a new identity, a fresh start, a new life, freedom from bondage. If we are going to be slaves to anything, it must be righteousness. Christ rules and reigns, not sin. Who we are or can become is completely wound up in the death, burial, and resurrection of Jesus Christ. It is how we identify ourselves and are identified. We can either be advocates for God and His purposes or for Satan and his. We have been given great grace.

Paul tells the Corinthian Church that where sin abounds, grace abounds doubly. God gives grace to overcome sin and temptations, but this new identity is not without responsibility. We are by no means perfect, and our identities and lives shouldn't be commanded by something that Christ has already defeated. We have a choice. We can be identified as agents of a sovereign God as we yield to His will, representatives of His nature, free as a result of His mercy and favor. We can be responsible, knowing that grace is not a pass to live without boundaries.

We are richly blessed by God. Romans 8:29 lets us know that we had *nothing* to do with His choosing us! In spite of ourselves, He has declared us righteous and has extended the invitation to commune with Him. Through Christ He has redeemed us. Through His Word He graciously shares His will and lets us know who we are to Him. No matter what others think of us, Colossians 3:12 reveals that we are "holy, and dearly loved."

We have to know who we are in Christ. We must be soberly aware of the great responsibility that comes along with our special identity. We are children of God. He hasn't been evasive about what He has done for us. Because of this alone, if anyone asks you who you are, you can honestly say that you are a new creation. You are a friend of God—greater still, a child of God.

CHAPTER 3

Stop Rushing, Patience is a Virtue

They have been quick to turn away from what I commanded them.

—Exodus 32:8

Woe ... to those who say, "Let God hurry; let him hasten his work so we may see it."

—Isaiah 5:18–19

Bear in mind that our Lord's patience means salvation.

—2 Peter 3:15

Considering frailty, a penchant for sin, and the vast difference between the sovereignty and majesty of the Creator and his creation, God's mindfulness of humankind is perplexing. Our mindfulness of God, however, can be woefully fickle. It is fascinating how immediately humans' thoughts turn to God, especially when there is a request or a need. A human being wants what he or she wants and wants it now. God's faithful nature guarantees that humankind is always on His mind, and the only issue that is urgent is our decision to be reconciled with God.

Why would the Lord even *bother* to acquaint himself with, or attend to *and* favor mankind? God made humanity, unlike all others, as creatures who could commune with God and see and acknowledge His love, kindness, generosity, and creativity. Do we slow down long enough to do so?

Unlike the angels, we were given souls, with which we feel, think, choose—and we are affected by God's goodness. We were made with the potential for being both earthly and divine. That God would be so consumed with thoughts of beings who may not honor, heed, or engage Him probably gave the ever-worshiping angels cause to wonder. Why would God create man with the propensity to fail *and* provide a way of escape from the fall? Did He know that many would neither acknowledge His merciful act nor take the time to thank Him for it? Why would you not want to thank someone who has done so much for you? More than you could even realize. I'll wait, until you finish thanking Him! Thank Him a little more!

The angels were made to serve, praise, worship, honor, and obey. No provisions were made for them. No promises were given. In fact, the arrogant angels who foolishly conspired against God and declared themselves His equals sparked a war in heaven and were ambushed by their own, cast out, and forever condemned. Mankind, however, received the mercy and grace of a faithful, loving God. Some angels were condemned for a single act, while mankind errs repeatedly, willfully, and without regard, yet God crafted a plan to declare humankind blameless. Does man ever soberly ponder this?

God sent His only begotten son to conquer death, hell, and the grave so that mankind would not have to answer for abysmal choices and abominable actions. It is mindboggling that God would not assign angels—consistent, faithful beings—to minister to mankind. Every possible provision has been made for mankind to be reconciled to God, and our response is minimal and very far from timely.

Being made in the likeness and the image of God does not exempt us from the grave necessity of being born again, and it only takes a moment to accomplish rebirth. Why do so many delay?

When we understand (as much as our finite minds can comprehend) who God is, then we can begin to grasp who we are, our purposes, and His expectations. Many find God's behavior odd, unnatural, weak, or manipulative. Perhaps that's why many choose not to believe— because, if given the chance to create, they would not have formed a being and lavished it with everything it could ever want and need without establishing strict rules of compliance. Free will would not have been in the blueprint! They would have created a robot of sorts— docile, predictable, obedient, and programmable. Who would create anything without a guarantee that it could be controlled and bound to follow implicit instructions? Who would continue to provide for someone who demonstrates indifference, lack of appreciation, and gross disrespect? God's ways are definitely not ours! He made humans without any mechanism to assure our compliance. Life and death were our choices. Common sense dictates the best choice. Yet God sought to force the hand of mankind at no time. It is a concept that is difficult to understand, but it inspires great gratitude in the heart of the believer. God knew His creation would not be able to live up to His standard of holiness and righteousness, yet He created us just the same. It behooves us, then, to consider the magnitude and intricacies of God's plan, see the depth of His love, and be thankful for His attentiveness. What's even more pitiful is how vile our souls would be without Him! We should carve out time in our schedules to listen and talk to God, to *be* with Him. What are we doing and how fast are we moving that we forget that there *is* no forward motion without God? There is no upward mobility, no haste to success.

We make an awful mistake when we attempt to negotiate this life at our own pace without God—especially when He reveals that we don't have to. When we choose any behavior, we also choose the consequences. Ignorance may be the given excuse, but it is never an acceptable one, nor does it lessen the effects of irresponsibility or willful misdeeds. Consequences are either deterrents or motivators. The choices we make can profit or condemn us. To be given a choice and still choose badly demonstrates that we are either unbelievably disoriented, fooled by an overinflated estimation of ourselves, in grave denial, reliant on luck, or so wounded and broken that we simply cease to care. Two choices were given—life or death. Why would anyone decide to take his chances? Many, unfortunately are accelerating toward eternal death, not eternal life, and don't know it. At the pinnacle is a place for God, and if we are rushing to do anything, we should rush to restore God to His rightful place in our lives.

When we choose the pace of life that makes room for God, I believe it makes His heart glad. He has such great plans for us! We should want to experience them! How wonderful is it to have heavenly beings assigned to us, watching over us as if we're royalty? The idea that the Son of God accepted an assignment that meant unbelievable suffering and a torturous death and didn't decide, after He rose, that His dealings with mankind were over, should make us rejoice continuously! We have angels ministering to us, a Savior daily advocating for us, and the spirit of the Lord literally taking up residence; guiding and leading us. How different our declarations and conversations should be! He is no proponent of favoritism, but God has so certainly favored mankind in every possible way! Faith and belief are the catalysts to confessions that demonstrate not only knowledge of what God has done, but thankfulness for it all.

God speaks life; what are you speaking and choosing? Are you speaking words of life that add value and color to the world around you, or are you speaking words of damnation that diminish your potential, discourage your soul, and breed darkness and defeat? With faith in God, it is effortless to speak life. It is faith in God's Word that allows us even to know that abundant living exists. When we say we have faith in God but speak idle words, our speech betrays us, and we expose ourselves to negativity, toil, lack, and poverty of soul. Wealth, in the material sense, without God, may as well be extreme poverty. Faith is the greatest currency ever established. Knowing God enables us to release anxiety, establish boundaries, set priorities, and realize how crucial it is to keep God front and center.

CHAPTER 4

Faith and Trust

Buy the truth and do not sell it—wisdom, instruction and insight as well.

—Proverbs 23:23

Guide me in your truth and teach me, for you are God my Savior, and my hope is in you all day long.

—Psalm 25:5

Jesus said, "I tell you the *truth*." If you can't trust the declarations of anyone else, you *can* trust the words of Jesus. He explained that faith is the key element to pleasing God, healing, wholeness, salvation, and so much more. Think about a mustard seed. It is extremely small. Ours is a "size matters" world, but the mustard seed isn't insecure at all! It is not the size of the seed that counts, but the faith of the seed! Imagine having the type of faith a mustard seed has! It appears insignificant. It is small. It is dwarfed by other seeds. It may be ignored by comparison. Its potential, however, encourages and motivates it and reminds it of what it will become! The mustard seed's faith allows it always to keep in mind that, though it may be tiny, it has the power and potential to be expansive, profitable, and mature. Seeing things from God's perspective and not superficially is so wonderful! The potential that a mustard seed has is enormous, not only in present possibilities, but in future abundance! It doesn't see itself as limited. It doesn't embrace doubt, question God, or become influenced by the reasoning, criticism, or ridicule of others. It knows what it is and what it is going to be! There is something on the inside that is nourishing, powerful, and miraculous! The seed knows that!

We have to embrace the same kind of assurance! The word of God is an excellent lenses through which we should see ourselves and others and appreciate our world. Our faith and trust is not in ourselves, but in the Word. Jesus is the Word of God, according to John 1:1. Having faith in God is having faith in His Word! John 1:14 tells us that the Word became flesh and took up residence among us. Perhaps the words written on tablets and scrolls were too difficult to comprehend. Perhaps people doubted the authenticity of the presentation. Maybe they thought it wasn't applicable to them or that they would never be able to conform. Living by the letter of the law meant sudden death for many. Imagine what a torturous way to live—knowing one's inclination to sin and inability to keep the whole law. God had to send Jesus! He had to give Himself! Mankind was doomed without Him! God made it clear that He did not send Christ to condemn the world. Salvation, redemption, restored relationship—these were God's objectives.

We tend to put our trust in what seems reasonable, make sense or at least somewhat consistent, and has a proven track record. It's easy to trust what you can see. It's easy to follow when you know where the leader is going. It's easy to comply when you have all the information and all your "Why?" questions are answered. Even if things don't look perfect, if you can look back and recall progress and success; your confidence won't be shaken. Trust isn't easy in the presence of doubt, fear, or anxiety. You want to know who's leading, what the orders are, and where the directions given are going to take you. You want to be safe; you don't want to suffer loss or feel insecure. Following the mandates of someone else can be a burden if you don't trust that person. Furthermore, nothing inspires more doubt than someone trying to get you to do something he has not successfully mastered himself! Jesus showed mankind that it was, in fact, possible to trust God, honor His requests, keep His law, and be diligent when it came to doing His will. God provided a perfect example. His Word became flesh. His Word came alive and went into action. Mankind could see the miracles. There were no tricks.

Perhaps some instructions do boggle the mind; perhaps there are times when we think, "God, are you sure?" Trust and faith are needed to erase the inclination to see God's word as some complicated code or collection of impossible demands. The natural mind regularly attempts to rationalize and even discourage us when it comes to Scripture. We trot out our logic and reason and make life in God impossible and unattainable. We misinterpret, argue, rewrite, rearrange, translate, justify, add to, and subtract from God's word. Unfortunately, our own lack of trust or misunderstanding causes us to confuse ourselves and others completely. Many people are led to false conversions, abandon the assembly of believers, and seek other religions and philosophies as a result of faulty teaching fueled by distrust in God's Word. Surely there must be some other requirement. Salvation can't possibly be so simple! God must have some other tough assignment, some lengthy procedure.

We portray a relationship with God as difficult. We project his Word as convoluted and mysterious. Subsequently, if one claims an inability to understand the Word, why should one feel compelled to follow it? Why not just boast in self-righteousness? Why not declare one's niceness, goodness, or attraction to good deeds—or at least one's efforts? Why not keep some of the law and skip the rest? Is the failure to completely trust God behind the campaign to categorize, compare, and contrast sin? Do we find ourselves in the Word, pat ourselves on the back for the things we are able to accomplish, and get stuck there? Are we still caught up in works alone because we simply cannot believe that God's plan and our acceptance of it are enough? Are we like the temple worshiper who was so arrogantly proud of his history of tithing but had no idea how to move the heart of God, commune with Him, and obtain mercy?

When we neglect to trust, believe, and have faith, we are in danger of basking in a false sense of entitlement, religious zeal, and skewed doctrine. It is a pitiful individual who fails to comprehend the need for God because of an overestimation of personal righteousness. It is an even more pitiful individual who relies on religiosity to determine the state of his heart, mind, and soul instead of exposing himself to the light of the Word of God. Paul was right. Dressed up or not, "filthy rags" is the perfect way to describe the handmade righteousness that lets us thumb our noses at others. What is humankind that God even bothers to pay attention? Is God as impressed with mankind as mankind is impressed with himself? Absolutely not! Look at man, preening, strutting, and heaping accolades upon himself, so sure that he is heaven-bound, so confident in his bylaws, denominational traditions, and churchy slogans and sayings—as if he could do anything apart from God! Imagine God shaking His revered head while saying, "I have to help him. The poor thing is so deluded."

We have to focus on God's righteousness—not on whether we eat or drink, dance or sit still, embrace bling or opt for plainness, speak in tongues or speak English, cut our hair or step on it, worship on Saturday or Sunday or Wednesday, or clap on two and four or one and three. God's righteousness is his Word, His will, His way, His requirement, and His promise, and it is sufficient for anyone! Why must we further complicate belief? Salvation is free! The call to fellowship with God has been given to "whosoever will"! Jesus has done the dirty work, and He said, "It is finished!" We can choose. Life, death, heaven, hell, fellowship, and separation are the options.

John 3:16 is so plain. His assurance, "You shall be saved," was not followed by any other stipulations. Why can't we simply trust God? Why can't we trust that He is more than acquainted with us, that He loves us, and that there are no hidden costs, detours, or mazes in His plan? All that is required is what He said. We can trust Him and His Word. It's not a game.

God's law is life! God loves deeply, faithfully, and consistently. He gave the world an opportunity to experience spiritual freedom. He is righteous, holy, without sin, and unchangeable, so there is nothing about His law that He despises or wishes to revise. He means every word of it, and noncompliance is not an option. Just because mankind was unable to follow the letter of the law didn't mean that God tossed it out. He made perfect provisions for mankind to avoid failure. He gave Himself! He did not come to take away the law; He came to fulfill it. The fulfillment of the law is the revelation of His love. If we love Him, then we will keep His commandments, not figure out a way to get around them or sin willfully to test His patience or veracity. God loves us all. We can be excited by the challenges of each day, confident of victory or circumstances, and create opportunities to grow in faith by trusting in what God says. Jesus said, "I tell you the truth."

CHAPTER 5

Faith and Thankfulness

Shout for joy to the Lord, all the earth. Worship the Lord with gladness; come before him with joyful songs. Know that the Lord is God. It is he who made us, and we are his. We are his people, the sheep of his pasture. Enter his gates with thanksgiving and his courts with praise; give thanks to him and praise his name. For the Lord is good and his love endures forever; his faithfulness continues through all generations.

—Psalm 100:1–5

Anyone with even a little home training knows how and when to say, "Thank you." Someone holds a door open for you, and you say, "Thank you." Someone picks up something you didn't know you dropped, then catches up with you and hands it to you. You say, "Thank you." Your meal arrives at your restaurant table, and it's exactly what you ordered, prepared just the way you like it. You say, "Thank you." You get a present for your wedding, birthday, anniversary, or perhaps no particular occasion. You reply with a cheerful "Thank you." Someone admires your suit or dress. You say, "Thank you." You didn't spin the cloth or make it with your own two hands; you just bought it, but you acknowledge that you've been complimented merely for the choice you made.

We probably say, "Thank you" for something every single day. We may give thanks for the most insignificant things, but our action is automatic. It's polite. It's the right response. We don't even think about it. We thank others when it is appropriate.

People don't have to be nice, efficient, thoughtful, helpful, or gracious. We don't always have to respond. Sometimes we don't. Sometimes we feel that we actually deserve the service, help, attention, and material comforts in our lives.

Some people proudly refer to themselves as *self-made*. They brag that no one ever helped them, gave them anything, or did anything for them. If you didn't know better, you'd think they gave birth to themselves! How is it that people forget that *any* help is still help, and God's grace and mercy cover us when we are not even thinking about them? All people, whether they admit it or not, have *something* for which they should be enthusiastically thankful. If you can't think of anything, think again.

If you've attended church for any length of time, you've heard someone say or sing, "When I think of the goodness of Jesus, and all He's done for me, my soul cries out, 'Hallelujah! Thank God for saving me!'" It's a common saying, but it should never become meaningless, trite, or insignificant. Thinking of God should inspire us to be grateful and full of thanks.

If you read the Book of Psalms, written by David, Asaph, Moses, and unnamed others, you'll see headings such as, "For the director of music," "A Psalm of David," "A Prayer of David," and "A song." You may even see the name of the tune to which the psalm should be sung. You may see the reason or circumstances in which the psalm was written. You may see what musical instruments are supposed to accompany the psalm. Many of the psalms let us know that the writer was in deep trouble, in despair, feeling alone, afraid, or in need of comfort. Psalm 100, however, is the only one where we see the heading, "A psalm for giving grateful praise." Notice how specific that is! Not just any kind of praise, but *grateful* praise. This is praise that's given with strength, vigor, affection, and intensity. The psalm is a rousing call to everyone to give thanks to God, and it tells the reasons why.

The psalm begins with these words: "Shout for joy to the Lord, all the earth." Shouting implies noise! We may think of ourselves as reserved and quiet, but this psalm challenges our reserve.

Read Psalm 66:8: "Praise our God, all peoples, let the sound of his praise be heard."

Psalm 98:4 also emphasizes exuberance: "Shout to the LORD, all the earth; break out in praise and sing for joy!"

There must be something to this attitude of praise!

"Worship the Lord with gladness" implies willingness, positive emotion, and a pleasant disposition. Next, "Come before him with joyful songs." There's nothing sad or flat about that advice! The songs shouldn't lull people to sleep—and they should be about God!

"Know that the Lord is God." It is important to know who you're praising! Whom are you singing about? You can't speak with any authority about a stranger! You have to be a credible witness. Knowing He is the one, true, and living God should inspire the content of your verbal praise and your songs. When you know who someone is, you're not vague about him, and you give him the credit, honor, hospitality, and service due.

"It is He who made us, and we are his; we are his people, the sheep of his pasture." Let's not get confused. Everything is all about Him! He's God, not us. He gets the glory! He's done all of the redemptive, creative, important, life-saving work! How dare we come into the churches that we call *God's houses* and forget that everything we do and say should direct people to God! How dare we put His name on the building and forget about God when we enter?

Are our churches merely shrines to men or Christian social clubs, or do we sincerely aim to come together to give thanks to our Creator?

"Enter his gates with thanksgiving and his courts with praise," wrote the psalmist. We should enter that mindset of praise and worship before we enter the parking lot! By the time we get to church, sitting down to be entertained, lectured, or exalted for what we have done should be the last thing on our minds. We should speak to God first before we address anyone else! After all, we came to offer thanks and praise to Him, didn't we?

Faith is not a denomination. It is not what we do. It is not a game of chance. It is a dynamic force, measurable and flexible, and when faith is nourished, it is a force with which to reckon. Faith is the substance, the necessary ingredient, the material that fuels our trust, hope, belief in, and dependence upon God. Faith is not fantasy or fiction, not is it frivolous. Nothing that God metes out is ever frivolous. Every ambition, goal, plan, and design is impotent and lifeless without faith. Faith inspires optimism and encourages high expectations. Faith is meant to be active; it is set to function, and it is already in place. It's not, however, going to jumpstart itself. It will quickly reveal what it is and isn't. It is not a bargaining chip. It is not a crystal ball. It is not a lottery ticket. Faith makes it plain and clear that God is real, alive, and present. Faith demonstrates the very existence of God. Faith backs up the unwavering assertion that God and His Word are true and that God is in control.

Lack of faith is detrimental to our spiritual well-being. Pleasing God is impossible without utilizing the tools He has so graciously given us. He distributes faith and fully expects us to exercise it. A lack of faith is evidenced by loss, brokenness, insufficiency, and inadequacy. Lack of faith causes us to compare ourselves to others and robs us of the peace God wants us to enjoy. Lack of faith inspires fear. There are so many things we could fear, but some of our fears are merely the results of our inability to trust God. The idea that we can't see our way to a solution or conclusion can be paralyzing. Fear, however, did not come from God.

Fear comes when faith is absent. The two elements cannot coexist. We are either full of fear or full of faith. As believers, we must live—not foolishly, but fearlessly—hoping in all things, believing in all things, and trusting in all things concerning God. Remove the fear, insert faith, and the possibilities for bold, forward motion become endless. Fear limits our lives. Fear coverts our spaces to cages. Faith in motion defies gravity and logic, defeats doubt, and invigorates belief.

Faith in God causes us to live lives of victory and limitless expectations. Every word that proceeds from the mouth of God is nourishment. There is no shortage. We are never in danger of running out. Faith is currency. Our thoughts and words—especially in prayer—should brim with faith. We don't have to see previews of the outcomes that God says are inevitable. The conditions don't have to be favorable. Prayer in faith is a sign of trust, and expectation is in each word.

Prayer in faith causes events and situations to materialize, improve, or resolve; it causes incorrect situations to be corrected. I think it makes God happy to know that we have confidence in Him. Faith is valuable and a guarantee. Knowing who God is and what He is capable of results from the faith He has given.

When you can see the results of what God has said and consistently experience His faithfulness over time, it is not difficult to trust Him and be thankful. It almost becomes second nature. Anxiety leaves. Worry dissipates. The need to take matters into one's own hands is a passing thought. Through faith, we know that God has covered every contingency. Nowhere is fear written into the plan for your life. When God promises to be with you always, there are no exceptions! Thank Him for it!

CHAPTER 6

God's Amazing Love Is Alive!

The love of God is abundant, present, overwhelming, and real! Come on say it with me " I am loved by God I will always be loved by God! With it, nothing is impossible for us. Love fulfills the law of God. Everything that is created is a reflection of God's love. His love can be found in the most seemingly insignificant things. Everything seems to testify to His presence, power, control, and creativity. What sets mankind apart is our ability to communicate with and about Him concerning the unique and marvelous world where we live.

We are human and divine, growing deeper into the divine image and nature of Christ and our words have power! Express your originality and release your personality as you shine in the truth of God's Word. That's right, God's words makes us shine as brightly as the stars in the sky. Some things we say startle us at times! We know that some of our declarations and observations did not originate as a result of our own educational or intellectual prowess. Some things are inspired, revealed, given, and directed by God Himself. The words that we speak can motivate or hinder, propel or bury. Our words are a testament to whether we trust and believe God or need to activate the measure of faith He has so graciously given. Understand that you can always be a part of a compelling purpose, continuously expecting the best in every situation!

The only thing that's difficult for God is lying and contradicting His own Word. It is truly impossible for Him to lie; He just can't do it.

It should not be difficult for us to trust someone who is incapable of being dishonest. We simply believe and agree with God, or we don't. The authority we have been given to ask anything in His name should be motivation enough to ask away—not foolishly or frivolously, but according to His will. If we remember that He only wants good things for us, it seems reasonable to just trust Him! He loves us!

God's name is love; He is love. How we stand with Him should matter. What He thinks of us doesn't have to be a mystery. When we see ourselves as He sees us, we will rid ourselves of the behavior that reveals whether we know Him, spend time with Him, and trust Him—or that we are banking on what we heard or gleaned from some temporary religious experience.

Being able to trust God and rely on His love empowers us to be able to tell or consult Him about anything! We have access! Whether it's debt, poverty, lack, drug addiction, soul ties, foolish agreements, unwise business deals, toxic relationships, terminal illness, employment decisions, children, purchases, travel, whatever—we have an attentive, loving heavenly Father who is well aware of our issues. Jesus said, "When you pray, say …" We have a loving God to whom we can speak! Understanding that approach means everything; we can talk ourselves right into His presence! There's nothing complicated or arcane about it. In His presence there's joy, fellowship, relief—and the meeting of needs.

What is it that binds us and keeps us from simply doing what God said—"casting our cares upon Him"? Has it been so long since we've talked to Him that we don't think He'll listen or remember us? That's the danger of assigning our own proclivities to Him. However, He's not petty, unforgiving, or small-minded.

Many are constrained by their choices, histories, habits, and thoughts; we can be tormented by reputations and secrets, haunted by insecurities, or trapped by those who forever keep our pasts alive. Many indict, disqualify, and imprison themselves and are resigned to their sense that they neither deserve nor expect God's love and help. If only we would consistently see ourselves in the light of His Word, we would never separate ourselves from someone who has given us a list of issues that will *never* come between us! Romans 8:38–39 is so clear! "For I am convinced that neither death, nor life, nor angels, nor principalities, nor things present, nor things to come, nor powers, nor height, nor depth, nor any other created thing, will be able to separate us from the love of God, which is in Christ Jesus our Lord." If those words don't convince us of how lovingly God considers us, how much He desires fellowship with us, and how eager He is to help us, I don't know what will. What is man that God is mindful of him? Man is the very apple of God's eye!

Armed with the love of God, you can tell the naysaying, tormenting spirit in your life that you are *not* the sum of your own mistakes, as you've been made to believe, possibly by yourself. God is the master of transforming the old and presenting it as a pristine new specimen. Proclaim liberty and the joy of being greatly loved. God loves you! Read the encouraging words of 1 John 4:16–17. "We have come to know and have believed the love which God has for us. God is love, and the one who abides in love abides in God, and God abides in him."

Gospel composer Andrae Crouch wrote a song, "I Don't Know Why Jesus Loves Me." The lyrics include these words: "I don't know why He cares. I don't know why He sacrificed His life. Oh, but I'm glad—so glad He did."

We don't understand the depth of God's love for us, but aren't we glad that He loves us? If we were to advise God, we'd probably tell Him what we would tell a friend: "Don't waste your time. Good riddance. They don't listen, don't act right, and are way too much trouble. If I were you, I would have dropped them a long time ago." Fortunately, however, we don't advise God. His love isn't fickle. We can simply thank and bless Him because we know we don't deserve His goodness. We have the privilege of simple gratitude.

We know ourselves. We know all that we've said and done. Other people know the things we've done that we don't even remember! God, on the other hand, will forget our repeated misdeeds and not even bring them up again! That's love! Paul said to the Christians at Corinth, "Love is the most excellent way to live wittingly!"

First Corinthians 13:4–7 states it clearly: "Love is patient, love is kind. It does not envy, it does not boast, it is not proud. It is not rude, it is not self-seeking, it is not easily provoked, it keeps no record of wrong. Love does not delight in evil, but rejoices with the truth. It always protects, always trusts, always hopes, always preserves. Love never fails!"

Fortunately for us, we don't have to understand God's love. All we have to do is accept it. Perhaps it is the acceptance of God's love that presents a problem for many people. We know how we behave, what we think, and what we would do. We have all had periods in our lives when forgiveness, reconciliation, and letting bygones be bygones seemed out of the question. We were determined to hold onto past hurts. We were unwilling to give certain people another chance ever again. We felt that we had every right to dislike or hate or hold a grudge. We've declared that when it comes to some people, we'd rather not be bothered anymore. Loving them was out of the question, and no one would blame us if we didn't.

God's ways are certainly not ours. Maybe we'd be more willing to accept God's unconditional love if we'd make every attempt to practice it ourselves.

God's love is a love we can all experience, and it is not based on our actions, but His attributes.

Read Romans 5:6–11 on God's love and its work of reconciliation.

> You see, at just the right time, when we were still powerless,
> Christ died for the ungodly. Very rarely will anyone die for
> a righteous person, though for a good person someone might

possibly dare to die. But God demonstrates his own love for us in this: While we were still sinners, Christ died for us. Since we have now been justified by his blood, how much more shall we be saved from God's wrath through him! For if, while we were God's enemies, we were reconciled to him through the death of his Son, how much more, having been reconciled, shall we be saved through his life! Not only is this so, but we also boast in God through our Lord Jesus Christ, through whom we have now received reconciliation.

Christ is a wonderful Savior who was sent by a loving God to do a work that no one else could do. Christ provided the penance, redemption, reparation, amends, payment, propitiation, recompense, redress, restitution, or satisfaction demanded by God for the sins of the whole world.

The passages from Paul's letter to the Romans underscore several crucial points. We were in a mess. God has always had a plan to get us out of our mess. God loves us and always has. Christ's sacrifice realized the reconciliation between fallen humankind and a holy God. Our belief in the Lord Jesus Christ provides for life everlasting in the presence of God.

Read Romans 5:18–21 on the huge impact of Christ's unique sacrifice.

Consequently, just as one trespass resulted in condemnation for all people, so also one righteous act resulted in justification and life for humankind. For just as through the disobedience of the one man the many were made sinners, so also through the obedience of the one man the many will be made righteous. The law was brought in so that the trespass might increase. But where sin increased, grace increased all the more, so that, just as sin reigned in death, so also grace might reign through righteousness to bring eternal life through Jesus Christ our Lord.

We don't like being blamed for what someone else has done. We really don't like being punished for what someone else has done. We definitely don't want to pay for someone else's mistakes.

Adam's sin created a horrible situation for humankind. Jesus took care of the debt. Imagine someone charging purchases on your credit card. You read the bill and figure that it couldn't be that much. They only charged one thing. Just when you think you only have to pay for what one criminal has done, you find out your card was used by millions of people.

No matter how you try to tell the credit card company that you didn't make any of the charges, what if they demand payment, and you're the one who have to pay the debt? What if you're innocent? but there is an obligation and an expectation. What if the credit card company knows you have the money and your check won't bounce. What if you can pay the debt in full? And what if as soon as your check clears, everyone— even the criminals—will find that their accounts are in good standing?

That is exactly what happened to Adam, Jesus took on the sin of Adam as well as every sin since. God so loved the world that there was only one person who satisfied God's requirement. There was only one suitable sacrifice. Christ was obedient and paid the debt that humanity owed. Fairness had nothing to do with it. It was all about love.

The wonderful grace that God has shown toward us seems too good to be true, but it is no gimmick. It wasn't an accident or a last-minute scheme. There are no tricks, and there's no fine print. God loves us, and we can rest assured that His love is true. Even though our sin rendered us guilty, unworthy, unrighteous, and totally deserving of God's displeasure, Christ's sacrifice offers us love, mercy, peace, and joy.

We can't allow anything to make us doubt God's love for us—not even ourselves. God is seriously committed to us.

Second Corinthians 11:2 solidifies how God feels: "I am jealous for you with a godly jealousy. I promised you to one husband, to Christ, so that I might present you as a pure virgin to him." No matter what we think of ourselves, we must consider ourselves the way God sees us.

Zechariah 2:8 uses the apple metaphor to show how precious God finds humankind: "For this is what the Lord Almighty says: "After the Glorious One has sent me against the nations that have plundered you—for whoever touches you touches the apple of his eye."

If you consider someone the apple of your eye, you regard that person as very special and precious. Imagine that. That's what God thinks of you! You are important to Him. He loves you.

This same love is also the topic in Jeremiah 31:3. "The Lord appeared to us in the past, saying: "I have loved you with an everlasting love; I have drawn you with unfailing kindness." When you read that passage, you need to know He's speaking directly to you! Yes, you.

Your personality, emotional condition, and behavior have no effect on God's love. God still loves you! Wherever you fit in, get in! God still loves you and wants you to know who you are in Him.

Read Psalm 8:4 to appreciate God's attentiveness. "What is mankind that you are mindful of them, human beings that you care for them?" Imagine that! God actually *thinks* about you!

Forget all the negative ways you describe yourself, and forget all the terms others might use to imply that you don't deserve God's love. We may be a lot of things, but we are not unloved by God! God didn't follow our plan or way. We tend to do good for those who we feel *deserve* it. Who has been good? Who has been naughty? That's how *we* determine what we will and won't do for others. We base it on how satisfactorily they have lived up to our expectations. We have a lot of nerve behaving this way because we haven't consistently lived up to *any* of God's expectations.

Romans 3:23 lets us know that *everyone* has sinned! No one has consistently pleased God. That is a sobering statement, and it is true. Even on our finest, most perfect days, we can't claim that we've done anything to deserve God's love, but we still have access to it!

Read Titus 3:4–6, which states that "the kindness and love of God our Savior toward man appeared, NOT by works of righteousness which WE have done, but according to HIS mercy he saved us, by the washing of regeneration, and renewing of the Holy Ghost."

Romans 5:6–8 lets us know how *pitiable* we were! In spite of ourselves, God loved us and demonstrated His love by offering His son Jesus as a ransom for us all. We've wronged God, yet He comes to us seeking reconciliation. Who does that? God does! We've done things that are worthy of death, yet God promises us everlasting life.

God loves us. Repeat that to yourself if you have to. Through Christ we have been justified!

We have a peace that surpasses all understanding. We have God's amazing grace and tender mercy. We can rejoice through tribulation; we have hope. We have the promise of the Holy Ghost. Our sins have been washed away and covered by the blood of Jesus. Although Adam's sin separated mankind from God, through Christ we have been reconciled. Does that mean we can live foolishly and aimlessly? Can we just do whatever we want? Sure. We have free will, but we should also remember that our actions have consequences. God loves us, but He is no pushover. Corrupt flesh can't inherit the kingdom of God. Unfortunately for some people, it takes affliction to make them focus their attention. Sometimes we think we're hurting others by our actions, but we're only hurting ourselves. God is perfectly able to redeem anyone!

In 1 Corinthians 5, the apostle Paul addresses immorality in the church. Someone had been behaving very badly. There was some sort of corruption taking place. The fifth verse is a little scary. Paul suggests that the church "hand this man over to Satan for the destruction of the flesh, so that his spirit may be saved on the day of the Lord."

Whatever was going on was so bad that Paul suggested someone be thrown out.

Notice, however, that nothing was said about God's love or grace being removed. Even those whom we consider the worst among us are not so bad that God cannot love and redeem them. Sometimes we don't want to give God that opportunity.

Modern-day psalmist David Curry wrote, "The safest place in the whole wide world is in the will of God." I would submit that the *worst* place is outside of His will. Why would we want to be at odds with God? Why would we want to be His enemies? Why would we want to know the degree of His wrath when He has done so much to demonstrate His love and grace? How much better is it to be a friend of God! There's a song we sing, though, and its words encourage us all: "To the utmost, Jesus saves. He will pick you up and turn you around. Hallelujah! Jesus saves."

Don't let anyone attach an amendment to what God has offered. Don't be fooled by extraneous man-made rules and requirements. When God declares His everlasting love, He means it without qualifications. There is no fine print that reads, "I'll love you if only or if you do this or that." All we have to do is accept the wonderful gift that God has provided.

How we live is a demonstration of our appreciation of our loving God. We ought to want to follow His way. We ought to want to please Him. Make no mistake, however. God's love is motivated purely by the fact that He *is* love, and His actions toward us were not based on our merits. Read 1 John 4:9, which states, "In this was manifested the love of God toward us, because that God sent his only begotten Son into the world, that we might live through him."

Ephesians 3:19 lets us know that the love of God surpasses all knowledge. We may never understand it, but that shouldn't keep us from acknowledging and accepting it. God's love is real and readily available to us all.

We were the angry, rebellious ones. God was consistent. We were the lost ones, unkind and unloving. God has been faithful. We needed redemption. God is holy. Considering our own state, the steps God has taken to demonstrate His love should be enough for us to accept His gift of salvation gladly and see the greatness of His patience and kindness. If we consider anything an act of God, declaring someone righteous and loving unconditionally should be at the top of the list. We can observe, experience, and participate in the love of God. It is real, alive and available to us all.

The very familiar passage of Scripture, John 3:16 should be all the verification that we need. "For God so loved the world that he gave his one and only Son, that whoever believes in him shall not perish but have eternal life."

CHAPTER 7

Motivated by Mercy

Turn from evil and do good; seek peace and pursue it.

—Psalm 34:14

Imagine having so much wealth that there's no room for you and someone else to remain in the same place. That was the case with Abram and Lot. How is it that we see things so differently? How do we fail to remember that our words and actions have consequences—not for the other person, but for us?

So many problems arise when people demand their own way, and those problems can spill over onto people who had nothing to do with the matter at all. Selfishness causes much strife in our lives. Many times people say words they shouldn't say. Words often spark physical confrontations. That's why we have to make sure our words are temperate. We can't afford to allow conflict to get out of hand. The guidance of God's Word will help us to solve conflicts for the benefit of all involved parties. Read Romans 14:19, which recommends a rational and evenhanded approach: "Let us therefore make every effort to do what leads to peace and to mutual edification." It really is possible to solve conflict without having your own way. Psalm 133:1 expresses the result: "Behold, how good and how pleasant it is for brothers to dwell together in unity!"

The word of God will show us that sometimes excesses in our lives can present problems. We do like win-win situations, but every issue will not end in our concept of victory. It's important that we concentrate on God's will, not our will. Sometimes, as in the case of Lot, we can think we're winning, and our seemingly clever and selfish choices can be our downfall and that of those around us.

Abraham lived for a time in the land of Canaan, traveled in Egypt, and ended up with wealth and honor, just as the children of Israel would eventually do. Chapters 11, 12, and 13 of the Book of Genesis reveal that Abraham was a generous and wealthy man. He shared the best of his land with his nephew Lot. Perhaps Abraham was so generous with Lot because he didn't think he would ever have a son of his own with his wife Sarah.

See what happens when we think? We forget what God promised! The Lord had instructed Abram to *leave* his family, but Lot, Lot's wife and daughters, *and* Lot's herdsmen trailed him. Abram moved extensively and eventually settled in the very places through which he had traveled. *The Complete Biblical Library Commentary* gives us insight on the lesson.

> Abram recognized that the continual controversy between the herdsmen could bring contention between him and Lot. He did not want that to happen, for they were "brothers," that is, close relatives. But, since there was not enough for all, he kindly suggested that they separate, each going a different way. Parting company would make it easier for them to find enough grass and water. Abram then told Lot to choose which direction he wanted to go. Abram did not have to do this. As the senior member of the group, he had the right to make that choice. Abram, who had been worshiping the Lord, was acting in faith, and trusting God. Like the Lord, he humbly and generously showed grace to his nephew Lot. Lot chose the green fields of the well-watered plain of the Jordan. This district between Jericho and Zoar was a tropical area, 800 to 1200 feet below sea level, where crops could grow all year-round. Like the rich delta of the Nile area

in Egypt, this well-watered land stretched to Zoar at the southeast end of the Dead Sea and reminded them of the garden of the Lord, the garden of Eden. Today, it no longer exists as a green, well-watered land. God's judgment on Sodom and Gomorrah brought a drastic change to the entire area. Abram was left on the dry hillsides of central Canaan, and Lot settled among the five cities of the plain, pitching his tent near Sodom. Zoar may be mentioned because it was probably a center of heathen worship. A temple has been discovered in that area; its steps were worn down by thousands of feet—probably by people coming from all five cities. Lot failed to look at the green fields around Sodom through God's eyes, however. Sodom was a center of all kinds of wickedness, that was evil in the sight of the Lord.

We all have had varying degrees of conflict in our lives. No one would think it unreasonable for you to look out for your own best interest. When conflicts arise that threaten our relationships with others, it's natural to want to salvage whatever we can, especially with people who are close to us. It would still feel better to us if our side wins, or if we're proven right. Being right, however, isn't always necessary. There are times when we seek compromise in an attempt to put out the fires in our lives. Sometimes it's just good to let people have, think, and do what they want. Sometimes there's just no need to discuss the issue or fight about it. As difficult as it may be, sometimes it's a good idea to stand down, put away your argument, forget about your rights, skip your point, and let others win. As we read about the conflict between Abram and Lot, his greedy nephew, we can definitely use them as examples of what to do and not do when we face conflicts. If we read Genesis 11:27–31 and Genesis 12:1–5, we can find out more about the relationship between Abraham and his nephew.

Genesis 13:1–7 tells of the family's migration.

> Then Abram went up from Egypt to the Negev—he, his wife, and all he had, and Lot with him. Abram was very rich in livestock, silver, and gold. He went by stages from

the Negev to Bethel, to the place between Bethel and Ai where his tent had formerly been, to the site where he had built the altar. And Abram called on the name of Yahweh there. Now Lot, who was traveling with Abram, also had flocks, herds, and tents. But the land was unable to support them as long as they stayed together, for they had so many possessions that they could not stay together, and there was quarreling between the herdsmen of Abram's livestock and the herdsmen of Lot's livestock. At that time, the Canaanites and the Perizzites were living in the land.

We can read Genesis 12:8 to find out what Abram was doing in Bethel and Genesis 12:10–20 to find out what he was doing in Egypt, what happened in his life, how he became wealthy, the level of his faith, and how much he depended on God.

It's interesting what can happen when you are only trying to do what seems correct. As we will see as we read Genesis 13:8–13, there's not always a solution that will satisfy everyone involved. Abraham made that effort.

Then Abram said to Lot, "Please, let's not have quarreling between you and me, or between your herdsmen and my herdsmen, since we are relatives. Isn't the whole land before you? Separate from me: if you go to the left, I will go to the right; if you go to the right, I will go to the left." Lot looked out and saw that the entire Jordan Valley as far as Zoar was well watered everywhere like the Lord's garden and the land of Egypt. This was before the Lord destroyed Sodom and Gomorrah. So Lot chose the entire Jordan Valley for himself. Then Lot journeyed eastward, and they separated from each other. Abram lived in the land of Canaan, but Lot lived in the cities of the valley and set up his tent near Sodom. Now, the men of Sodom were evil—sinning greatly against the Lord.

Isn't it interesting where Lot chose to live? Think about the place he chose to take his wife and daughters. He obviously was not thinking about the example he was setting or the environment to which he was taking his family. Love and wisdom did not motivate him. He didn't even seem to be bothered about separating from his blessed uncle. The last thing Abraham wanted, however, was an argument. Notice how he stated the obvious. Should you ever have to remind your relatives that you are related? Did Lot forget those family ties as he greedily scoped out the best land for himself?

What do you think was on Abraham's mind as he sought to resolve the problem? You can always tell when people are interested in resolving an issue and when they are content for the confusion to continue. We must work to avoid conflict as diligently as we can.

Sometimes, to eliminate conflict, it's best to separate amicably and prayerfully for a time, knowing that the Lord is always expecting us to behave in a way that is pleasing to Him. We have to avoid saying anything that would make reconciliation impossible. Read Proverbs 15:1, which advises us, "A soft answer turns away wrath: but grievous words stir up anger."

In Genesis 13:8–13, Abraham's story continues.

> After Lot had separated from him, the Lord said to Abram, "Look from the place where you are. Look north and south, east and west, for I will give you and your offspring forever all the land that you see. I will make your offspring like the dust of the earth, so that if anyone could count the dust of the earth, then your offspring could be counted. Get up and walk around the land, through its length and width, for I will give it to you." So Abram moved his tent and went to live near the oaks of Mamre at Hebron, where he built an altar to the Lord.

Rest assured that the promises God has made to you have *nothing* to do with what others do or say. Your faith in God is crucial. What He tells you to do, where He tells you to go, and your obedience to His commands are all critical. Your worship is vital. Notice how Abraham worshiped the Lord no matter where he was! Abraham was blessed. Is it possible that our lives are blessed because of the promises that God made to someone else? Is it possible that Lot never realized that his relationship with Abraham was more than just that of uncle and nephew, but the source of any grace he had been shown? Sometimes we really do mistreat the wrong people.

When conflict and strife are protracted, relationships are strained and troubled, and people who are not even involved find themselves entangled. We have to embrace an attitude of meekness, maturity, and strength. We must let God's way be our guide. Even if others don't want to cooperate, we must always show our readiness for reconciliation and peace. Think about it. If you decide to be gracious, peace-loving, and unselfish, would God be bothered by that? Would God be angry at you if you know that someone has taken advantage of you, but you refuse to retaliate or argue? Would He think that you were weak? Would He decide to have nothing to do with you? Of course not!

Remember His promise to you. Seeking God first is the best way to resolve conflict. Seeking our own way is the best way to keep conflict alive.

We can't allow anyone whose moral standards are impaired or low to determine how we behave. We have to know that our choices in life do have consequences.

Save yourself the stress of conflict with others. Choose peace. Be motivated by mercy and trust God to handle all the details. His resolution will be perfect.

As it is expressed in Psalm 16:11, "You make known to me the path of life; you will fill me with joy in your presence, with eternal pleasures at your right hand."

There are some conversations, activities, and plans from which you should be quite grateful to be excluded. When discernment makes those scenarios unmistakably clear, you'll breathe a sigh of relief. You will then be even more thankful that you're right where you are. You'll even thank God for the joy and contentment brought by genuine people and endeavors. Less work, no financial investment, peace, reduced stress, and saved time are the results of appreciating the grass on your side of the fence and not falling for the artificial turf someone else has put down on his side to feel better about himself.

You have to be happy with yourself. Too many people are making declarations that backfire and show just how unhappy they really are.

You can't make someone wish to be part of an endeavor, especially if you can't make that person believe that you are enjoying it yourself! Perhaps that's the source of many people's frustration. Perhaps that's why many are so busy at being *busy*. They're desperately trying to get attention and responses from people they don't even like or from those they see as competitors.

It is paramount to have contentment—to be appreciative and know just how blessed you really are.

CHAPTER 8

Working for God

Whose purpose or need do you and your specific skills suit best? To whom do you and your professional activity belong? Where do you apply your talents, skills, and expertise? Whose instructions, rules, requirements, or standards do you follow each day to achieve goals? For whom do you work? A better question is, "For whom *should* you work?"

The relationship between Jacob and Laban, partly found in chapter 31 of Genesis, is an excellent study in miscommunication and workplace frustration. Read Genesis 31:38–42. Jacob is the narrator of this story.

> I have been with you for twenty years now. Your sheep and goats have not miscarried, nor have I eaten rams from your flocks. I did not bring you animals torn by wild beasts; I bore the loss myself—and you demanded payment from me for whatever was stolen by day or night. This was my situation: The heat consumed me in the daytime, and the cold at night, and sleep fled from my eyes. It was like this for the twenty years I was in your household. I worked for you fourteen years for your two daughters, and six years for your flocks, and you changed my wages ten times.

Jacob certainly sounded like a disgruntled employee! He had kept a mental log of his employment history. Also on his mind were unsafe working conditions and unreasonable demands. Most people would have quit. Why didn't he? Usually, when people put up with foolishness, there's some kind of payoff. What do people stand to gain for dealing with bad conditions at work?

The years on his job caused a noticeable change in Jacob's attitude. He was no longer the agreeable, eager, and happy person he had been.

Consider Genesis 29:10: "When Jacob saw Rachel daughter of his uncle Laban, and Laban's sheep, he went over and rolled the stone away from the mouth of the well, and watered his uncle's sheep."

Notice that Jacob didn't have any help, and he didn't *ask* for any. There were other people around, but he jumped right in and got the job done. He hadn't filled out an application or been briefed on the job description. He didn't complain about how much the stone weighed or how many sheep needed water. He didn't demand to be paid. He just went to work. *Someone* motivated him to volunteer his time and energy, and her name was Rachel. Make no mistake—the work would have been done whether he was there or not, but Jacob *wanted* something, and his actions were not merely to be helpful.

Isn't it remarkable how doing what you *want* to do makes you totally forget about everything else? You're not tired, hungry, bored, or worried about what you have to do later.

Genesis 29:20 continues the story. "So Jacob served seven years to get Rachel, but they seemed like only a few days to him because of his love for her."

If you read on, you'll discover that Jacob didn't exactly get what he wanted out of the deal. While he was busy ogling Rachel, he didn't read the fine print of his deal with Laban. It's important to know what you're getting into before you commit to any task. You don't want to be so gullible, deceived, or distracted that you end up in a complicated mess and can't readily get out of it. In Genesis 31:42, Jacob reproaches Laban: "If the God of my father, the God of Abraham and the Fear of Isaac, had not been with me, you would surely have sent me away empty-handed. But God has seen my hardship and the toil of my hands, and last night he rebuked you."

Jacob has realized, at this point, that his boss has a boss. It's sad when an employer or employee has to be shamed, forced, or frightened into doing right. Even though Jacob was not *completely* innocent, and his motives were not the purest, God still didn't allow Laban to take total advantage of him. One of the saddest parts of the story is that Jacob and Laban were relatives.

Jacob waited twenty years to tell his uncle Laban what he thought of him. He had agreed to work with no real idea who he was working *for*. Laban was a shady character, and Jacob, in dealing with him, got a taste of his own medicine. Jacob worked according to his contract, which could be considered admirable. Over time, his attitude toward his work became less admirable. He obviously believed, though, that the reward was worth the aggravation.

He soon found out that even the beautiful Rachel had some issues. I imagine that we all come to a point when we wonder if our plans and the anticipated rewards for our labor are actually as wonderful as we once thought.

No one likes to feel obligated or forced to do anything, particularly if they feel cheated or misused. Jacob had a goal and worked diligently and happily for it. Upon finding out that he had been blindsided by a technicality, he had a decision to make—he could keep working and get what he wanted or quit. He wasn't the least bit happy about the arrangements of his second round of employment, but he wanted something very badly, so he agreed to Laban's terms. His activity was no longer motivated by a desire to do a good job. If we were to assess his attitude on the job, we'd probably conclude that he had lost his original enthusiasm. In addition, he no longer trusted his employer. Jacob and Laban didn't exactly like each other. When they said, "May the LORD watch between me and thee, when we are absent one from another," they meant that God's omniscient eye saw both of them. We should let God evaluate our honesty. We can trust Him.

It is always best to know the contractual details in the work you do. Misunderstandings and outright deceit can lead to bitterness on the job. It's good to be able to respect those who have authority over you. It's good to know and understand what's expected of you. It's also good to know all the details of payment when the work is done. I would not recommend that anyone do any job that person does not want to do, but we all know that people do so all the time. Some people should decline certain assignments before carelessness, lack of work ethic, or a negative attitude threatens to ruin a potentially pleasant working environment or damage a project.

There's no need to shuffle or grin in the face of a supervisor. There's no need to sow seeds of discord. Sometimes it's best to leave a job to someone else. At least it will get done without unnecessary grief. This is no endorsement of childish behavior, laziness, divisiveness, stubbornness, or failure to assume responsibility. We've already seen the scripture that highlights the consequences of deliberate inactivity, Thessalonians 3:10: "The one who is unwilling to work shall not eat."

Does that mean that we should engage in work no matter how we feel about it? Do our feelings even matter? If they affect how we carry out specific tasks, how do we resolve that effect? Should we take on just any old job, whether we are suited for it or not? Most people aren't fans of poverty, so off to work they go. There are some tasks we have to do, so we brave the cold, heat, and traffic and work to sustain ourselves and our families. Many of us do just that every day, despite our personal feelings. Misery on the job, however, is obviously bad for us.

I am always happy for people who do work they love and are adequately paid. On the other hand, there are those who, as soon as they open their eyes in the morning, begin complaining about their impending daily tasks. Everything is a chore. Everything is drudgery. Everything is stressful. Everything is either too time-consuming or a waste of time. Those who hear the whining shake their heads and wonder, "If it's so bad, why do they do it? Why do they continue to torture themselves?" The answer is usually very simple. People need money or whatever reward is exchanged for their labor.

How many people would leave their current positions in a heartbeat if they suddenly found themselves independently wealthy? Would the people closest to you be surprised to know that you'd much rather be doing something else, with someone else, and for someone else?

Is it even possible to maintain a cheerful, mature, conscientious attitude while engaged in activities that simply aren't appealing anymore? How we feel about our work is just as important as the work itself. The difference between mediocrity and excellence is often found in the attitude of the worker. We've heard that "attitude is everything," and attitude can also be the difference between staying on the job and walking away.

Assignments carried out under a cloud of fear may get done, but over time, morale will diminish. Assignments completed out of necessity or grudgingly may get done, too, but the work environment may be a toxic one.

How do we rise above negativity and our own feelings and do the work assigned to us in an excellent way? The answer lies in changing our motivational perspective.

When we embrace the notion that our chief supervisor is God, it may be a lot easier—even a delight—to get up, go to work, and do not just a fair job, according to the letter of the law, but a superior job—which may inspire others to do the same.

On the same job, some people will decide that nothing is worth the stress, and they will walk away from opportunities that others wish they had.

Every work environment would be so much more productive, safe, respectful, and fair if everyone—employers and employees—would keep a few points in mind:

1. God is the ultimate boss, and He is watching, evaluating, and rewarding.
2. On the job, no matter what your position may be, your aim should be to please God.
3. As a supervisor, manager, CEO, or employer, you are still accountable to a higher authority.

Can you imagine how work would be if we did everything as if it depended on God's approval? Imagine the results we could have if everyone simply concentrated on doing the best job possible, regardless of who was watching! Consider the workplace harmony that would be possible if people thought before they spoke, considered the impact of their actions, and gave others the respect and consideration due to every human being.

Read Proverbs 15:1 on the subject of conciliatory speech: "A soft answer turneth away wrath: but grievous words stir up anger." And stirring up anger is undesirable because angry people don't generally make the best workers.

Proverbs 11:17–18 emphasizes the advantage of kindness: "Those who are kind benefit themselves—but the cruel bring ruin on themselves. A wicked person earns deceptive wages, but the one who sows righteousness reaps a sure reward."

We have to know that God's approval of our words and actions is more valuable than anything man can offer. What's the point in having a job, the money that comes along with it, and the toys that the money can buy if God is not pleased with any of it—or with us? We should take our guidance from Romans 12:2. "Do not conform to the pattern of this world, but be transformed by the renewing of your mind. Then you will be able to test and approve what God's will is—his good, pleasing and perfect will."

Whether we are subordinates or supervisors, it's up to us to decide whether we will take our tasks seriously, maintain our productivity, care about the caliber of our output, and employ godly principles while on the job. How we regard others is something we must resolve as well. Favoritism, a frequent workplace issue, works to no one's advantage.

Acts 10:34 comments on this issue. "Then Peter began to speak: 'I now realize how true it is that God does not show favoritism.'" Romans 2:11 seconds that: "For God does not show favoritism." James 2:9 puts the same matter in legalistic terms: "But if you show favoritism, you sin and are convicted by the law as lawbreakers."

Imagine the impact if those passages of Scripture were posted on the walls of every workplace. How you feel about a person will govern how you treat that individual. If you see someone as inferior, it's only a matter of time before you resort to disrespectful behavior, insensitive words, and unreasonable demands. If you regard others as superior, it will distract you from focusing on what pleases God and compel you to do whatever is necessary to please the people you've exalted.

We should instead consider the message of Galatians 1:10: "Am I now trying to win the approval of human beings, or of God? Or, am I trying to please people? If I were still trying to please people, I would not be a servant of Christ."

When God's approval is the aim of everyone on the job, no matter what positions people hold, they will be able to function with ease. Leaders who follow God care not only about the product, but about the people who produce it. It's easy to follow when there's God-conscious, effective, competent, and considerate leadership.

Hebrews 13:17 comments on authority: "Have confidence in your leaders and submit to their authority, because they keep watch over you as those who must give an account. Do this so that their work will be a joy, not a burden, for that would be of no benefit to you."

Both groups win when workers and supervisors are primarily concerned about pleasing God in everything they do. We would all be wise to follow the lead of Jesus. If we want to know how to glorify God, our divine employer, one way is found in John 17:4: "I have brought you glory on earth by finishing the work you gave me to do."

God shows all the characteristics of a great employer. He creates and sustains a good work environment. He lets us know that we are important and valuable and that the assignment He has given us is important. He aims to cultivate our fullest potential. He emphasizes the importance of balance in our lives. He compensates us well, gives us benefits, and institutes excellent policies and practices.

He develops great leaders who are good at managing people. His Word records the efforts of those whose achievements He appreciates. Through his Word, He has established and communicated standards for integrity and ethical behavior. He is concerned about the impact His product and workers have on the community. When making decisions, He considers the cost and does what will benefit us all.

Colossians 3:23 describes our work as an offering to God: "Work willingly at whatever you do, as though you were working for the Lord rather than for people."

Who are you working for? Decide today that you work for God. That choice will make a difference in your attitude, your work ethic, the atmosphere of your workplace, and the outcome of every task.

CHAPTER 9

Our Helper!

Back in the early 1950s, the Davis Sisters recorded a song titled, "Get Right with God." I think the best line in the song is "He will show you how."

Imagine someone demanding that you do something, giving you instructions on how to do it, and then carrying out the work *for* you. "Down at the Cross, where he shed his blood" is not a haphazard phrase. At the cross, mankind got the greatest assistance from Jesus. Getting right with God was not something we could have ever done on our own—and God *knew* it. Jesus said, "I am the way, the truth, and the life, no man can come to the father, but by me."

"Therefore, if anyone is in Christ, the new creation has come: The old has gone, the new is here!"

The key is to be "in Christ." Tragically, unnecessarily, some people try to accomplish work of this kind on their own. God knows who we are. He made us. He also desires fellowship with us. He wants us to be like Him. At the beginning, mankind was made in God's image and likeness, but sin separated us from the presence of God. We have ALWAYS had divine help at our disposal. The prophet Samuel wrote, "You, Lord, are my lamp; the Lord turns my darkness into light. With your help I can advance against a troop; with my God I can scale a wall."

Now, no one is telling *you* to go outside and run headlong into a barricade or break your neck by leaping off your roof. God didn't tell you to do that—but when He *does* instruct us to do His will, our ability to succeed won't be by our might or for our glory, but HIS.

Galatians 5:22–23 advises us on the sweet fruits of the Spirit: "But the fruit of the Spirit is love, joy, peace, forbearance, kindness, goodness, faithfulness, gentleness and self-control. Against such things there is no law."

The sinful nature of mankind is incapable of manifesting the fruit of the Spirit. God knew that. Paul wrote that the sinful nature is a slave to the law of sin! The sacrifice of Christ has delivered us—if we are going to be slaves to anything, it should be God's law!

I can't repeat it enough: We have to know just how important the plan of salvation is in our lives. We can't just gloss over it. We can't just drag it out on Resurrection Sunday, and then pack it away for the rest of the year. The death, burial, and resurrection of Christ should be always before us, reminding us daily of the huge danger and condemnation from which God rescued us. We have to believe we needed His help. When we share Christ with others, we can't possibly overemphasize that it is His Spirit working in us.

His power helps us want to do His will each day, every hour, even every second. It is HIS finished work—not ours—that helps us the most. It's His work that we should boast about. We have no ability to obey without Him! We have to point people to the *true* helper and know that we cannot navigate this Christian journey without Him.

First Corinthians 1:18 comments on the safety belief offers believers: "For the message of the cross is foolishness to those who are perishing, but to us who are being saved it is the power of God."

When you are drowning, you don't care what the boat looks like, how old the life preserver is, or the nationality of the person who throws you a rope. All you care about is staying alive. When you get on dry land and tell the story, you don't talk about how well you floated, or how swiftly you could swim, or who else might have come along to save you if you had waited a little while. You talk about and celebrate being *alive*! You talk about that saving experience. You talk about how people you didn't even know used their resources, strength, and time and cared enough to pluck you out of the water. You show your appreciation to those who pulled you to safety. You may even tell the story over and over! You hope not to be in the same jeopardy again. You learned that you don't like drowning, but you sure do like knowing that help comes in the nick of time.

From the beginning, God established the concept of helping. If God says we need help, it shows that He knows something that we don't. The wonderful thing is that He provided us with a way to have a relationship with Him, but many times we look for the shortcut. Remember Cain's sacrifice? He knew what God required, so why was he mad when God rejected his offering? God told him to do what was right. He told Cain that sin desired to have him, but he must rule over it. Instead of accepting the help, Cain took offense, and the consequences were tragic. Sometimes we're so busy focusing on the wrong thing that we miss out on the help we could get to act properly.

"Help" is God's idea and part of His plan. You've heard the saying, "Good help is hard to find." That's not true. Good help is *always* available! Here are the pertinent questions.

1. Do we know help when we see it?
2. Do we reject help because it doesn't look or arrive as we want it to?
3. Are we too stubborn or prideful to accept help?
4. Have we believed the lie that we don't deserve help or need it?
5. Have we allowed someone with an agenda to persuade us to refuse help?

Sometimes we develop a Lone Ranger mentality. We get the crazy idea that we live our lives all on our own. We don't need or take instruction, correction, or advice. We know it all. Remember how Cain asked the Lord, "Am I my brother's keeper?" He was being a smart aleck. God already knew what he had done. Cain rejected God's helpful advice concerning his offering; in his jealousy, he plotted and killed his brother. He and his brother had two different occupations. Their offerings were never going to be the same, but the requirements for a pleasing sacrifice applied to both of them. Cain was afraid that his brother's offering would be better. What was stopping him from trying harder? He figured that God wouldn't have anything to compare if Abel wasn't around and that then he could be top dog. We know when we're doing our best and when we're slacking.

We don't like seeing our inefficiency exposed, but God can't lie. Nothing reveals our own laziness and stubbornness more than when we see competence and excellence rewarded. Instead of taking the helpful advice that would encourage his improvement, Cain took his incompetence out on Abel.

We can't just do what we want, the way we want, and expect God to be pleased—especially when He has told us what He wants us to do and has provided the help to do it.

Sometimes we behave and speak as if we had created ourselves. Why should we ever accept help from anyone? Thinking like this leaves God out of the equation and creates a self-righteous, judgmental spirit that is void of humility. It is this same spirit that overtook Lucifer, who began to see himself as God's equal. That's the attitude that got him kicked out of Heaven—"I'm great all by myself. I don't need help. I don't need God."

Sometimes our wrongdoing keeps us from asking for the help that we need. We all have wronged God many times, and we often feel we have no right to ask Him for anything. At times we fear that our sin will cause Him to reject us. That kind of thinking goes against His Word.

Even our prayers sometimes demonstrate that we don't trust God or really know Him. We address Him as if He is an important stranger or a distant friend. We approach Him fearfully, as if we're making a deal with a loan shark. Many people fail to approach Him at all.

Think about the people who are close to you. The old saying goes, "Birds of a feather flock together." Sin is a powerful separator on one hand, and it draws and unites on the other. Do you socialize with a person because of that person's honesty or his or her troublemaking tendencies? Think of the people you avoid. Do you avoid them because they can expose your wrongdoing, or is it because they encourage you to do the right thing?

Think of God's predicament. A holy God has nothing in common with sinful man. Sin repels and insults God. Why has He bothered to help us?

He came up with a life-giving solution that drew us *closer* to Him.

John 3:16 reminds us how greatly God loves us. Helping us has always been His plan. He continues to point us toward Jesus, our advocate and redeemer. It's a shame to have help available and refuse to take advantage of it.

Why continue stumbling around in the dark when we can walk in the light? We have help!

In Genesis 2:18, God said that man shouldn't be alone, so He made him a helpmeet. When Eve gave birth to Cain, she acknowledged God's help. God told Moses and Aaron that He would help them speak and tell them what to do. Helpfulness originated with God, and in order to live a godly life, we need all the help we can get—from God and each other.

Galatians 6:8 elaborates on Spirit over self: "Whoever sows to please their flesh, from the flesh will reap destruction; whoever sows to please the Spirit, from the Spirit will reap eternal life."

That's pretty explicit. This Christian life is completely hopeless without God's help. It is just religion and exercise without God's help. The enemy would love it if we start thinking that God's help is unnecessary or unavailable. When God's way seems too hard, people come up with religious rules, ideas, plans, traditions, and practices that they think they can successfully follow. They expect God to endorse them. Then they dump these unreasonable, burdensome standards on others, and no one succeeds—including the people who established the standards in the first place. We spend so much time trying to fix people with our ways, according to our human nature. We think we're helping, but when our help is apart from God's ideal, we will make things worse every time.

God made man a certain way. Humankind's essential qualities were not corrupt in the beginning. God and Adam had perfect fellowship. Adam disobeyed and plunged mankind into darkness. God then worked out a way that humanity could be restored to communion with Him. The Creator mercifully helped His creation. He was the only one who could help sufficiently. We have to know that our help still comes from God and that no one is too high or low to receive it.

In his message titled, "Watch Them Dogs," Rev. B. W. Smith said, "It ain't no easier for a preacher to get to heaven than it is for you. We all trying to just make it in."

In 1 Peter 4:18, we are advised of our delicate position: "And if the righteous are barely saved, what will become of the godless and wicked?" We can't become complacent and think that right living is of our own making or is a result of our good deeds, church attendance, or the size of our offerings.

Nothing we can offer, do, or say is more effective than the sacrifice of Christ. It is up to us to accept it and believe. He loves us, and He is ready to help us. Why won't we ask?

Luke 15:21–24 concludes the famous story of the Prodigal Son. The Prodigal Son realizes his error and confesses it.

> The son said to him, "Father, I have sinned against heaven and against you. I am no longer worthy to be called your son." But the father said to his servants, "Quick! Bring the best robe and put it on him. Put a ring on his finger and sandals on his feet. Bring the fattened calf and kill it. Let's have a feast and celebrate. For this son of mine was dead and is alive again; he was lost and is found." So they began to celebrate.

The son was not expecting that kind of response! He knew what his father's possessions were. Sadly, however, for whatever reason, he wasn't sure of his father's love. Expecting his father to be cold, mean, and indifferent, he had gone back home. Look at the way he approached his father. He came ready to bargain. He acted like a servant or a hired hand. The way his father responded to him affected his brother's reaction too. His brother was actually upset that his father welcomed him! He wasn't happy that his brother was home at all!

Sometimes we show that we aren't happy when God gives help and love to those we consider undeserving. We don't want God to help certain people because we don't think they're as worthy as we are. We often come to God as if we are slaves, not His sons and daughters. How we feel about ourselves, past experiences, and our own thinking will determine whether we will ask God—or anyone—for help. God knows everything that we have done. When we didn't deserve his grace, God recovered us. He didn't leave us estranged. He accepted us with love. He redeemed us and, through the sacrifice of Christ, sought to give us the opportunity to gain the right standing in him that Adam lost in the garden.

God helped us get back to Him. Righteousness is a free gift. We are able now to commune with God without an overwhelming sense of failure and shame. Righteousness guarantees us fellowship with God. It is not, however, a pass. We need God's help in the battle with sin. Our wisdom is useless. We can try, but we could not and cannot successfully deal with sin-sickness with our own wisdom.

Read Proverbs 21:21 on the pursuit of righteousness: "Whoever pursues righteousness and love finds life, prosperity and honor." What better reflects prosperity than being a son or daughter of the most high God? What can be more honorable?

Left to our own devices, we are doomed to failure. Ephesians 2:3–5 goes into detail about sin and the stagnation it brings.

> It wasn't so long ago that you were mired in that old stagnant life of sin. You let the world, which doesn't know the first thing about living, tell you how to live. You filled your lungs with polluted unbelief, and then exhaled disobedience. We all did it, all of us doing what we felt like doing, when we felt like doing it, all of us in the same boat. It's a wonder God didn't lose his temper and do away with the whole lot of us. Instead, immense in mercy, and with an incredible love, he embraced us. He took our sin-dead lives and made us alive in Christ. He did all this on his own, with no help from us! Then he picked us up and set us down in highest heaven in company with Jesus, our Messiah.

God's will is holy. It is right. Our will is contrary and divided. God's help is thorough and secure. We need God's help! The apostle Paul, in his writings, helps us to see just how inadequate and frustrating the law is as a way for maintaining the right standing with God. Legalistic thinking will not maintain that standard for us because there is something flawed in the character of mankind. The flaw stems from our original fall into sin. The law, with all its serious consequences and prohibitions, still fails at times to control human behavior. People do what they want even when right and wrong are apparent. The Holy Ghost is in us as believers, but we are not completely transformed. To maintain our correct standing with God and to avoid confusion, every day we must acknowledge God and demonstrate gratitude because God helps us achieve goals we could never have reached by ourselves.

What we believe and how deeply we trust God is crucial. Jesus was under a lot of stress; as apprehensive as He was, however, He was not confused. We can be skeptical, scatterbrained, and misled on many points but not about our relationship with God or His promises and willingness to help us. The Message Bible translation of 1 John 5:14–15 explains how to avoid confusion on this point: "My purpose in writing is simply this: that you who believe in God's Son will know beyond the shadow of a doubt that you have eternal life—the reality and not the illusion."

The Bible emphasizes how bold and free we can be in the presence of God. It stresses how freely we can ask and how sure we can be that He's listening when we ask according to His will in Jesus' name. We don't have to wonder; we can be confident that He hears us. The Holy Ghost resides in us and endows us with power. It is what we need every second, minute, and hour of each day. Because we believe in the risen Christ, we are His sons and daughters; we are God's children and joint heirs with Jesus.

We can call on Him just as a child should be able to call on a good parent. We don't have to be timid or afraid to approach Him.

Romans 8:26–27 advises us about prayer.

> And the Holy Spirit helps us in our weakness. For example, we don't know what God wants us to pray for. But the Holy Spirit prays for us with groanings that cannot be expressed in words. And the Father, who knows all hearts, knows what the Spirit is saying—for the Spirit pleads for us believers in harmony with God's own will.

Imagine that! Even when we don't what kind of help to ask for and can't put our needs into words, God makes a way once again! God has no difficulty translating. When we are overwhelmed, He takes that burden upon Himself and helps us. Our weakness is replaced by the Spirit's power.

The Holy Spirit is part of the godhead, acquainted with the very mind of God. Without doubt, the Spirit's deep and earnest intercession for us will accord with God's will and not our own. We have help to live. We have help to pray. We couldn't earn that help, and we didn't deserve it, but we have divine help to live this life. That's good news. It should make us all the more willing to help one another.

CHAPTER 10

Rest

It is useless for you for you to work so hard from early morning until late at night, anxiously working for food to eat; for God gives rest to his loved ones.

—Psalm 127:2

Rest awaits those who trust and obey! God promises this rest to those who enter through faith and reverence, through believing and acting on His Word. This is not a one-time act of good conscience, as some may think, such as starting to attend church, reading the Bible, and being what we consider *nice* to people. There are some who try to change by doing what they think is good or right in their own eyes or by connecting a string of positive actions. Their hope is in their actions, but will it change the course of their lives just because they have decided to do right? This type of self-righteousness can and does, in the long run, bring greater stress into an individual's life. Life does not take a turn for the better when faith is rooted improperly in works, not in obedience to the Word of God. Direction that comes from God's Word ends in rest and peace, success and prosperity. Only God has power and control over life and its course. Everything that happens is allowed or not allowed by God. We may never know why He allows some events, good or bad, to happen in our lives, or why He does not allow others, which we may need badly, to happen. It is certain that God's ways are not like our ways.

Isaiah 55:8–9 is a great reminder of the difference between human thoughts and divine thoughts. "'For my thoughts are not your thoughts, neither are your ways my ways,' declares the LORD. 'As the heavens are higher than the earth, so are my ways higher than your ways and my thoughts than your thoughts.'"

We can have rest and peace in the worst of situations, even if we cannot understand what is going on in our lives, if we believe in God. That means that we believe that He will work our situation out for our benefit. We will come out of our difficulties much improved if we trust God and accept what He has allowed or not allowed.

God has offered us all the opportunity to enter into His rest.

In the Old Testament, God gave the Israelites the opportunity to enter a new promised land, but they failed to enter because of disobedience to and distrust of God, whose instructions were channeled through His servant Moses. Today God offers all the world the chance to enter His utopia by believing in the Lord Jesus, the Christ who saves us by His anointing.

This may be hard for some to understand. However, remember that all you have to do is believe!

The works of the flesh can look like God's divine directions at times. How can we identify these times? When an action flows from God's divine direction, its outcome benefits you. Even if the actual conditions of your life do not change, you experience joy. This joy cannot derive from people or external things, but from internal confidence that brings forth hope in God and from obedience to the instructions and commands of God. From such obedience comes an overwhelming joy that is unquenchable, springing up into everlasting life. You will see a crystal-clear vision of your own destiny. Greater still is the abundant joy that ignites others! With this assurance, we do not allow distractions, even bodily pains, sickness, or fear to prevent us from following divine directions. To be part of a body is to help with building up the body of Christ. It is not a stressful chore, but a continuous joy.

Colossians 3:23 is a great reminder of the enthusiasm we should summon for our work. "Whatever you do, do your work heartily, as for the Lord rather than for men."

It is the Lord we aim to please, but surely we know that God doesn't need us to do anything for Him. We really should listen to Him, though, as we pile more onto our plates than we can handle. Rest was God's idea.

Sometimes we act as if we are doing God favors by initiating all kinds of projects and campaigns. We busy ourselves and expect blessings in return, as if we have some kind of barter agreement with God. We boast, "I read my Bible every day. I pray. I start my day with God. I go to church regularly." We should not expect any prizes if these actions are all just for show.

Rested, refreshed people who have peace of mind have no desire to trade places with people who are not experiencing the rest and joy of the Lord. They are not tricked into feeling guilty; they know when to stop and take the rest offered by God. Many people work harder just before a vacation or before they finish a project or assignment because a rest period is coming.

Although many of our projects may be admirable, they pale in comparison to what we should boast about if we're going to boast at all. As it is written in 1 Corinthians 1:31, "Let the one who boasts boast in the Lord." Romans 4:2 also includes a comment about boasting, referring to Abraham: "If his good deeds had made him acceptable to God, he would have had something to boast about. But that was not God's way."

Our efforts should be profitable to the Kingdom of God, not burdensome or full of stress to jeopardize our health and relationships. Keep focused on spiritual significance.

In His command to rest, God has given us an incredible gift and blessing. In many ways, however, we have turned even the Sabbath into a work day. Some people seem to feel that they haven't really accomplished anything good unless they're exhausted at day's end. Are their efforts really for God and His purposes or for themselves? We should take time, be quiet, and listen intently to what God has to say. Are we doing all the talking when we talk to God, with emphasis on what we want and need so that we can revert to our endless activity?

Do we really spend quality time with God? Is what we call our "devotional" or worship time just something else to do, or is it a viable, important aspect of our lives and investment in personal growth? Are we truly communing with God as we read and study His Word, or are we just collecting more trivia? Is God really pleased with us and our nonstop lifestyle? Have we ever bothered to ask Him to show us how to rest in Him through faith and trust, or are we unwilling to give up our schedules? Are we afraid that He might put an end to the activities we cherish the most?

When you truly rest, you honor God. Do you want to honor God? Then you need to rest. Do we really get quiet enough to listen to God and spend time at His feet, on our knees, humbling ourselves before our righteous God? If we did, we'd brag much less about our numerous activities. We'd caution ourselves before boasting and realize just how much help we needed and received as a result of the finished work of Christ on Calvary.

In Psalm 91:1, the psalmist writes of the comfort of rest: "He that dwelleth in the shelter of the Most High, will rest in the shadow of the Almighty."

In *The Treasury of David*, Charles Spurgeon wrote about the Christian's fellowship with God.

> The blessings here promised are not for all believers, but for those who live in close fellowship with God. Every child of God looks towards the inner sanctuary and the mercy-seat, yet all do not dwell in the most holy place; they run to it at times, and enjoy occasional approaches, but they do not habitually reside in the mysterious presence. Those who, through rich grace obtain unusual and continuous communion with God, so as to abide in Christ, and Christ in them, become possessors of rare and special benefits, which are missed by those who follow from afar off, and grieve the Holy Spirit of God. Into the secret place is where those only who know the love of God in Christ Jesus come. They dwell there to live in Christ by faith. Under The Almighty himself, is where his shadow is, and hence those who dwell in his secret place are shielded by Him.

Isn't that where *we* want to be? How do we get so busy that we don't even think we have time to rest?

Traditions play a big role in what we consider prayer, praise, and worship. They also play a role in how we view God and adhere to His Word. Even as we gather to worship, how focused are we when it's time to hear the Word? We're blessed to have pastors, priests, and leaders who stay in the presence of God to hear Him and to deliver that message of hope and peace to our souls. They are the men or women whom God has sent as the shepherds of His earthly flock. While some are so busy with their lives, these men and women commune with God in prayer on their behalf. They study, counsel, and minister to us, and God speaks to us through them. Why is it that some churchgoers are listening, learning, and growing in God through these messages while others dissect, criticize, ignore, or reject them? So consumed with criticality, they don't hear from God or His servants and thereby miss out on ways to enjoy rest and enrich their lives. Read Hebrews 13:17, in which we are advised to accept the authority of pastors: "Have confidence in your leaders and submit to their authority, because they keep watch over you as those who must give an account. Do this so that their work will be a joy, not a burden, for that would be of no benefit to you."

One negative way to be busy is being busy with loose chatter. Are we busy murmuring as Miriam and Aaron did against Moses? Read Numbers 12:1–9, which relates the frightening consequences of such talk.

> Miriam and Aaron began to talk against Moses because of his Cushite wife, for he had married a Cushite.
>
> "Has the Lord spoken only through Moses?" they asked. "Hasn't he also spoken through us?" And the Lord heard this. Now Moses was a very humble man, more humble than anyone else on the face of the earth. At once, the Lord said to Moses, Aaron and Miriam, "Come out to the tent of meeting, all three of you." So, the three of them went out. Then the Lord came down in a pillar of cloud; he stood at the entrance to the tent and summoned Aaron and Miriam. When the two of them stepped forward, he said, "Listen to my words: When there is a prophet among you, I, the Lord, reveal myself to them in visions, I speak to them in dreams. But this is not true of my servant Moses; he is faithful in all my house. With him I speak face to face, clearly and not in riddles; he sees the form of the Lord. Why then were you not afraid to speak against my servant Moses?" The anger of the Lord burned against them, and he left them.

God hears *everything* we say. He hears how we regard our activities and abilities. He knows whether we keep ourselves diligent and industrious.

Rest doesn't always imply lounging or sleep. There are times when we simply need to ease up, slow down, and take a break from anything and everything that would impede or impair our relationship with God. Sometimes getting the rest we need is as easy as saying, "No." We have to learn how to set boundaries, guard our time, and know our strengths and weaknesses. Don't be so busy fulfilling other people's agendas that you have no time for God, your families, or yourselves.

Does our concern about our church community truly manifest itself in service? Or do we sometimes create work for ourselves by involving ourselves in situations where our involvement may be inappropriate? Instead of seeking such involvement, we should set aside time to spend with our immediate families or alone. We need balance. Lack of balance causes us to be ungrateful or demanding when we should be thankful and appreciative. Imbalance causes us to be critical and divisive when we should be encouraging and cooperative; it keeps us from being truthful and sincere.

What do you need to stop doing, if only for a time, to be refreshed? What business in your life needs a rest so that you can rest too? God offers us an opportunity to refresh ourselves. He suggests it. He recommends it, yet many of us are still trying to earn our keep by being busy.

Our quandary is particularly sad when we are busy with religion, but not with our relationship with God. In the Word of God, we can find ourselves; we can recover. Our advice to do so is in Matthew 11:29: "Take my yoke upon you and learn from me, for I am gentle and humble in heart, and you will find rest for your souls."

In my opinion, *Gentle* means to be mildly temperament in our behavior, displaying kindness. I see it as moderate in our actions, soft in impact, not being harsh or severe toward others. To be gentle is to *Humble* one's self, showing or having a low key or modest esteem of self and having a low estimate of one's own importance. We can be very important and humbly gentle at the same time. I believe that meekness does not mean weekness.

Jesus was meek, though also assertive when necessary, and respectful. He was neither proud nor arrogant. He calls us to learn from His example. Mark 6:30–31 gives an account of Jesus calling a halt to busyness.

> The apostles gathered around Jesus and reported to him all they had done and taught. Then, because so many people were coming and going that they did not even have a chance to eat, he said to them, "Come with me by yourselves to a quiet place and get some rest."

What did Jesus tell them to do? Rest! The story continues in verses 32–34.

> So they went away by themselves in a boat to a solitary place. But many who saw them leaving recognized them and ran on foot from all the towns and got there ahead of them. When Jesus landed and saw a large crowd, he had compassion on them, because they were like sheep without a shepherd. So he began teaching them many things.

Who was teaching? Who was working? *Jesus* was! What was the multitude doing? They were listening and learning. Was anyone complaining? No! What were His disciples supposed to be doing? Watching and resting! The familiar story continues in verses 35–44.

> By this time it was late in the day, so his disciples came to him. "This is a remote place," they said, "and it's already very late. Send the people away so that they can go to the surrounding countryside and villages and buy themselves something to eat." But he answered, "You give them something to eat." They said to him, "That would take more than half a year's wages! Are we to go and spend that much on bread and give it to them to eat?" "How many loaves do you have?" he asked. "Go and see." When they found out, they said, "Five—and two fish." Then Jesus directed them to have all the people sit down in groups on the green grass. So they sat down in groups of hundreds and fifties. Taking the five loaves and the two fish and looking up to heaven, he gave thanks and broke the loaves. Then he gave them to his disciples to distribute to the people. He also divided the two fish among them all. They all ate and were satisfied, and the disciples picked up twelve basketfuls of broken pieces of

bread and fish. The number of the men who had eaten was five thousand.

There's a difference between idleness and rest. With a well-defined agenda, God specifically set aside the Sabbath. The story is told in Exodus 31:12–18.

> The LORD spoke to Moses, saying, "But as for you, speak to the sons of Israel, saying, "You shall surely observe My sabbaths; for this is a sign between Me and you throughout your generations, that you may know that I am the LORD who sanctifies you. Therefore you are to observe the sabbath, for it is holy to you. Everyone who profanes it shall surely be put to death; for whoever does any work on it, that person shall be cut off from among his people. For six days work may be done, but on the seventh day there is a sabbath of complete rest, holy to the LORD; whoever does any work on the sabbath day shall surely be put to death." So the sons of Israel shall observe the sabbath, to celebrate the sabbath throughout their generations as a perpetual covenant. It is a sign between Me and the sons of Israel forever; for in six days the LORD made heaven and earth, but on the seventh day He ceased from labor, and was refreshed. When He had finished speaking with him upon Mount Sinai, He gave Moses the two tablets of the testimony, tablets of stone, written by the finger of God.

The word *sabbath* appears about 126 times in the Bible. Was the keeping of the Sabbath reserved only for Old Testament Israelites, or does it apply to us as well?

The Bible refers to "solemn rest," and "a holy day." Keeping the Sabbath was not a suggestion to the Children of Israel, but a command. God created the Sabbath to be kept forever by those who believe. Do you believe? Do you keep it? Can we afford to dispense with the customs that God ordains for our benefit and rest?

Think about how you spend the Sabbath. Whether you observe it on the seventh day of the week or the first day, are you resting? Are you communing with God?

The first time we actually see the term *sabbath* in the Bible is in Exodus 16:21–30. It aligns with God blessing His people with manna from on high. God instructed the Children of Israel while they were in the wilderness. Notice that He delivered no manna on the seventh day, but gave the people a double portion on the sixth day. God demonstrated the standard. From the beginning, He has done so. He rested, and not because He was exhausted—God doesn't need sleep.

What if everyone spent the Sabbath reading, studying, and meditating on and listening to the Word of God? What peace, love, and unity families around this world would experience! What a novel idea!

Let's endeavor to understand what service really means, keeping in mind that rest is an integral part of service. Let's be sure about our calling and purpose, always remembering that we can be so much more effective if we obey God and rest. Let us aim to be still enough to hear the voice of God and follow His divine direction for our lives. He rested. Since He is our example, we too should rest. Take a rest!

Jesus' words in Matthew 11:28–30 were, "Come to me, all you who are weary and burdened, and I will give you rest."

CHAPTER 11

Damage Control

It is impossible for those who have once been enlightened, who have tasted the heavenly gift, who have shared in the Holy Spirit, who have tasted the goodness of the word of God and the powers of the coming age and who have fallen away, to be brought back to repentance. To their loss they are crucifying the Son of God all over again and subjecting him to public disgrace.

—Hebrews 6:4–6

Do not be anxious about anything, but in every situation, by prayer and petition, with thanksgiving, present your requests to God.

—Philippians 4:6

Is it possible for professing believers to make the church look bad in the eyes of the world? Has the reputation of the church suffered beyond repair? In this "keeping it real" generation, professing men and women are found to keep embarrassing, shocking, contradictory, hypocritical, and unholy notions when it comes to the church. Bad examples of Christianity give society more reasons to reject God, His word, and houses of worship. Some say, "See, that's why I don't even go to church," with great frequency, not because God has failed but because many of His professing representatives aren't representing Him or His kingdom particularly well. This, however, is no excuse for the average lay person or churchgoer to abandon the faith.

The body of Christ, the visible church, is discredited when poor decisions made by leaders in private are revealed in public. It is ironic that these leaders, who know what they are doing while sinning, look for compassion and understanding after being caught in the act or exposed. They would have done better to confess their pathological practices, repent, and realign their lives with the Word of God. It is hypocritical to the max to tell others to trust God and then demonstrate that one does not trust God through the evidence of an unholy lifestyle. "Do as I say, not as I do!" is ineffective advice. A true Christian, whether leader or follower, will be empowered by the Holy Spirit to demonstrate righteousness through his or her lifestyle as well as by proclamation. In 2 Peter 1:10, we are advised, "So, dear brothers and sisters, work hard to prove that you really are among those God has called and chosen. Do these things, and you will never fall away."

There were many men and women who lived in faith, from the Old Testament times until now—not perfect, but holy! You and I can do it too. God will keep those who keep their eyes on Him, no matter what. It is important to study the Word of God for ourselves. No one has to be misled, confused, or unsettled by events or by negativity toward the church. Technology has thrown open the windows and doors of the church as never before. The Internet allows us to discover everything, and everything is *not* putting its best foot forward. Sometimes, as members of the church, we discover information that makes us cringe and shake our heads. That's no excuse to give up. More good deeds than bad ones are done in the name of the Lord. Perhaps we should ask ourselves what we are doing to help advance God's kingdom and whether our own lives help or hurt the the church.

The Bible is still a bestseller, still revered all over the world, and still the living Word of God. Jesus' name is still exalted. He is still praised and honored, and souls are still being won! Relax. God's Word remains powerful and prevails.

At times I have seen that people who treat their enemies wrongly or fail to adhere to their standard of Christian living sometimes do not *want* God to be so merciful to those they criticize. They wanted God to punish everyone who is not behaving in a manner that they deem godly. God is certainly patient with all of us. There shouldn't be a sweeping indictment of the *entire* Body of Christ simply because of the actions of a handful of people. If we want to see drama, we don't even have to look that far. The local church, from the pulpit to the door, has historically provided enough ungodly activity to keep a writer busy forever. Why? Because it is populated by imperfect *people*, and people are simply fascinating! We have to be careful, though, with our assessments of the lives of others. We can't ever forget what we had to be delivered from, and how patient God was with each of us. We have to remember that, by the grace of God, salvation came to us all. Therefore, let us never lack compassion, patience, kindness, mercy, and love toward others.

God has the capacity to change hearts and minds. Fortunately, it's not up to us to decide when, how, or if He does it or not. The next time someone falls, fails, acts out, contradicts, compromises, sells out, messes up, misspeaks, misquotes, or mishandles some situation, opt for a good Christian response. Pray for that person. This requires you to pray also for yourself so you can have the power to help an erring brother or sister. Am I my brother's keeper? Yes, we all are our brothers' keepers.

CHAPTER 12

Self-searching

You have searched me, Lord, and you know me. You know when I sit and when I rise; you perceive my thoughts from afar. You discern my going out and my lying down; you are familiar with all my ways. Before a word is on my tongue you, Lord, know it completely.

—Psalm 139:1–4

You don't realize God is all you truly need until God is all you have left. At times God will allow events to break you down until you slow down and complete a self-audit. Take an inventory of how your life is playing out then. When the common denominator is you, everyone else can't always be at fault. Sometimes our own choices, issues, and motives have to be thoroughly examined, apart from anything someone else did or said to offend us. At times, because of your own egocentricity, you may have to lose everything to find out that God's plan for your life includes all you will ever need and desire!

The word of God is a true mirror to the soul of man. Perhaps that's why some don't like to look into the Bible as much as others do. God's mirror, the Bible, is not like the image-altering mirror at a circus or amusement park; it will not change your image so you can look better than you are or to amuse you. However, it will amaze you by showing you just how much you need God's help. It will not only show you what you look like, but also what you are doing, whether right or wrong.

Some people want to know what they are doing wrong so that they can put it right. Others don't want to see or know what is wrong with their actions. Some might say that it might be good to allow someone to tell you about yourself without interruption because that might help a person improve. I disagree. Only the Word of God can accurately judge the thoughts and attitudes of the heart. God sees everything, knows everything, and uncovers everything in time. All the other ways we seek to improve ourselves or draw new people to us when our old friends have had enough of us can never hide a damaged personality or bitter heart.

All human faults and misbehaviors are exposed before God. The list includes self-centeredness, dishonesty, manipulativeness, whining, neediness, inconsistency, abusiveness, and demanding or controlling behavior. Of course we want the love, respect, and admiration of the people who prove they actually care, but even they can tolerate only so much negativity. Even family members get tired sometimes and declare, "Enough is enough."

No one wants to be surrounded by yes-men and users who are expert at bowing, scraping, dancing around facts and truths, and general dishonesty. Sometimes the person who walks away is deemed uncommitted, disloyal, foolish, or stupid. However, sometimes people walk away after heavy introspection and a decision not to be part of someone else's negativity or confusion. Maybe the person who walked away was not the troubled one. Maybe that person didn't say what someone else wanted to hear because of being too busy in self-praise to listen. Maybe that person who walked away knew that no one would listen and saved his or her breath.

It is painful to look at yourself and see behaviors or attitudes that need to be corrected, but to remain unable to reach them. In this "I'm gonna be me, narcissistic culture, it is worth the effort to take a closer look at self, if positive change is the goal.

"This is just the way I am," shouldn't be an excuse to mistreat others or expect them to understand mistreatment or consent to it.

Sometimes we're so busy getting a point across that we don't see how offensive, annoying, divisive, abrasive, childish, narrow-minded, selfish, judgmental, arrogant, insecure, and unfair we can be! It's good to feel that your life plan is working out, but what's going on when no one is looking except God and you?

Who are we really, when no one is watching us? What is our character like when there is nothing to prove to anyone? We have to go back and address messes made, issues glossed over, mishandled people, lies, situations manipulated to make someone else look bad, and seeds of discord. Take a good look at yourself; self-introspection can have a direct effect on everything you're trying to accomplish.

Find out what others actually want and like. Remember that what you want and like is not of paramount importance to all! We should take the time to care and listen to people rather than pushing what we think to be the truth. As long as being right is more important than what *is* right, we may win arguments but lose the one in which we are trying to convince with truth. There is a reason why we grant limited or no access to some people. Sometimes we decide that we have no reason and no desire to put up with some individuals.

If you treat people right, you won't have to wonder about them; they will enjoy your presence and let you know that they do. If you treat *yourself* right, you won't hook-up or connect with people who make you feel worse about yourself than you should. Self-searching examines one's own heart, not others' hearts. If we judge ourselves, we do not greatly need others' judgment. If we would correct ourselves by the revelation of the Word of God, our lives would reveal more love, peace, joy, and faith. Growing in God's grace, our hearts would contribute to the quality of the relationships in our lives. God is poised to shine His light on our situations—and *nothing* will escape His scrutiny. We move from mercy to grace, from grace to greater grace, and from God's greater grace to His overwhelming glory in our lives. Thank God that He does not rate us according to our worldly status and titles, but by the attitudes of our hearts!

CHAPTER 13

Consider the Truth

And the Word became flesh and dwelt among us, and we beheld His glory, the glory as of the only begotten of the Father, full of grace and truth.

—John 1:14

All truth is measured by *the* truth, and He walked in human form on the earth as clear evidence of God's love, good intentions, and peace for all men. That is truth! God's goodness overshadows our badness. His righteousness overshadows our sinfulness. God is greater than humanity. No matter how low a man falls, God will pick him up when he calls on the name of the Lord. There is always reason to have hope when you know Jesus and His intention to help you, no matter what you've experienced or done.

Remember that the Bible says, "For when we were still without strength, in due time Christ died for the ungodly … But God demonstrates His own love toward us, in that while we were still sinners, Christ died for us."

Not after we got our act together, but while we were errant and confused, God came to our rescue by sending Jesus, whose name means *Jehovah is salvation*, to die in our place and erase the sins of all who put their faith and trust in His virgin birth, sinless life, death, burial, and resurrection with all power (authority) in His hands. If God does this for the sinner, if He did this for you and me when we were living in sin, think of what He will do for the one who becomes a Christian through belief! Think of what He will do for you and what He has done for you. Better still, thank Him for all that He has done for you!

Jesus died for us. It is interesting how people process information they've been given. One of the most important aspects of learning is knowing how and where to look for accurate, relevant information and then knowing what to do with it. I realize that people learn differently, and something valuable can be learned from everyone—even through people with whom one has no ties. No matter how differently we learn, it is good to have as much information as possible before we form opinions, judgments, and decisions or even have intelligent discussions.

Some people need to ask many questions, and there's nothing wrong with that. I often say there's no stupid question, but sometimes we pose safe, tame questions that won't raise eyebrows or challenge accepted ideas. At times we worry that our questions will start an argument or make us sound as if we lack intelligence or prudence in our judgment; perhaps we feel stupid. Sometimes we do a lot of talking that won't get us any closer to the answers we need. Sometimes we make comments that we think will impress others.

Sometimes we ask questions purely for our own edification or peace of mind. Sometimes we're fishing for information that's really none of our business. Sometimes, unfortunately, we fail to ask at all because we don't want the responsibility that comes with having certain information. Once you have knowledge, you have no excuse for ignoring it. You have to deal with that information.

When it comes to our lives and our places in God's plan, there are questions that will afford us the answers we really need. Are we brave enough to ask those questions and accept the truth? Do we posture, delude ourselves, or remain in the dark to escape the truth? Do we really want the truth, and from whom are we willing to receive it? Are we all sanctified, declared holy, and dedicated to God, or is that just for some people? Do our actions matter? What does God think? What's the truth?

Truth can be defined by a dictionary as conformity to fact or actuality. It is sincerity, reality, integrity, or fidelity to an original or standard. Is that what we really want? Jesus said, "Thy word is truth," as he prayed to the Father in John 17:17.

Psalm 139:23–24 reveals the anxiety that can come with an earnest search for truth. "Search me, God, and know my heart; test me and know my anxious thoughts," wrote the psalmist. "See if there is any offensive way in me, and lead me in the way everlasting."

That's quite a prayer request. If you sincerely prayed that prayer, as David did, would you accept what God revealed? Would you even dare pray like that?

In the final courtroom scene of the 1992 film, *A Few Good Men*, the judge shouted, "Consider yourself in contempt!" as the prosecuting attorney risked his career to question a high-ranking witness.

"Did you order the Code Red?" the attorney demanded. The judge told the witness, who was a colonel, that he didn't have to answer, but the colonel was so angry and arrogant that he told the judge he would answer anyway. The colonel shouted, "You want answers?" The attorney shouted back, "I want the truth!"

How many times do we fail to seek answers because we are afraid of what we will find out? How many times do we press an issue because we already know what the reality is and just want it confirmed or exposed? Could the colonel's low evaluation of the attorney apply to us? Are we unable to handle the truth? Is there information we think is best left unknown? God knows everything. Do we think we're sparing or protecting others by not being forthcoming with information? On the other hand, could the attorney's evaluation of the colonel apply to us? Are we hiding something? Do we hold onto the truth and only tell it when we're up against a wall or angry? Do we think we're above the law? Do we manipulate information in our own favor?

Is the truth too much for us to handle, so we decide it's not good for others either? Is the truth reserved for special people, while others get bits and pieces of information? Just how do we reason and process information concerning others and ourselves? Is every life important and sacred, or are some people dispensable and undeserving of truth, rights, honesty, or integrity? God know how we think. When we are wrong—and we are often wrong—who's going to tell us?

We can't always count on people to be honest with us. For various reasons, even within the closest personal relationships, some information is deliberately withheld. Perhaps we feel that others won't hear us. Perhaps we feel that they won't appreciate the truth. Perhaps we are afraid of the consequences. Perhaps we believe the truth won't do any good or bring any positive change. Revelation does come with responsibility, but how selective should we be?

We can't always anticipate what others are going to do with the truth. The truth has caused some good men and the greatest of men to die. But the truth also sets us free! The validity, helpfulness, and quality of the information you get depends on who you ask for it. If you want the truth, you don't ask a known liar.

If you want the truth, you also don't ask someone who wishes you harm or is in competition with you. If you want the truth, you don't ask someone who cares more about keeping a position or reward than being considered honest. If you want the truth, you don't ask someone who is fearful of retaliation. Some people don't mind if you are deceived. Sadly, some people don't seem to mind being deceived either. Hosea 4:6 reminds us that a lack of knowledge or wisdom or an outright rejection of God's Word and way are all destructive.

As a matter of fact, ignorance or rejection of knowledge works out best for some people. The less they know, the better off they think they are. Ignorance, though, never has been and never will be a good excuse.

The truth comes from those who genuinely care, are well-informed, and don't want you stumbling around in the dark. For a famous statement on truth, read the words of Jesus as recorded in John 8:31–32: "If you continue in My word, then you are truly disciples of Mine; and you will know the truth, and the truth will make you free."

Proverbs 10:21 also contains wisdom about truth: "The lips of the righteous nourish many, but fools die for lack of sense."

Only someone who values you will dare to tell you the truth, though we don't always accept it with gratitude.

The truth doesn't always support personal agendas, political affiliations, or individual preferences. The truth is not always convenient. It may not support our evaluation of ourselves, but it is as necessary as air for our physical, mental, emotional, and spiritual development. Our very lives depend on the truth, so we can't be afraid to seek God even if it means we have to make difficult changes in our thinking and practices.

When seeking the truth about others, we can be as diligent as Sherlock Holmes. We will turn over every stone and investigate every tiny lead. Even the media that is responsible for providing information, may be of little help. Some respected news outlets have become no better than gossip columns. With some reporters, being the first to tell a story has become more important than reporting accurate information. We want nothing less than full disclosure and transparency when it comes to other people, especially leaders. When it comes to the truth about ourselves, however, we aren't nearly as eager for the truth to be known. When it comes to our own lives, we want discretion, mercy, respect, and privacy.

For every truth that others think they know about us, we know more. God, on the other hand, knows all.

In Deuteronomy 32:4, the perfection of God is detailed: "The works of God are perfect, and all his ways are judgments: God is faithful and without any iniquity, he is just and right."

Psalm 33:4 also expounds on God and truth: "For the word of the Lord is right; and all his works are done in truth."

God doesn't need any other authority to back up His Word. He is truth and is therefore incapable of lying.

In Psalm 139, we find David addressing God and seeking truth. He could give us some pointers on how to ask for the truth and whom we should ask. He knows that God is not clueless, stupid, or moved by flattery. He's aware that he is not speaking to someone who does not know him. He goes beyond merely citing how good God is. He's not just flattering God. He's almost reminding himself of what he knows about God because there's something else that he wants to know. David reveals his own wonder concerning God's attributes. He gets right to the point and eagerly wants God to do something that we, too, should desire. He addresses God directly and asks Him to investigate his life. There's another request coming later, and David wants to feel justified in asking God to act on his behalf.

In Psalm 139:1–6, David praises the scope of God's knowledge.

> You have searched me, Lord, and you know me. You know when I sit and when I rise; you perceive my thoughts from afar. You discern my going out, and my lying down; you are familiar with all my ways. Before a word is on my tongue you, Lord, know it completely. You hem me in—behind and before—and you lay your hand upon me. Such knowledge is too wonderful for me; too lofty for me to attain.

Having said all this, David continues. He respects God as an authority over his own life. God won't lie to him. He is prepared for whatever God has to say.

In Psalm 139:13–16, David extends this theme,

> For you created my inmost being; you knit me together in my mother's womb. I praise you because I am fearfully and wonderfully made; your works are wonderful, I know that full well. My frame was not hidden from you when I was made in the secret place, when I was woven together in the depths of the earth. Your eyes saw my unformed body; all the days ordained for me were written in your book before one of them came to be.

David wrote with trust and confidence. Was David being complimentary, poetic, or prophetic? Was he expressing praise or distress? Was his florid assessment of God for a purpose?

Yes. David was reminding both God and himself of their extensive, supernatural relationship. David essentially acknowledged that God knew him intimately and in great detail! He knew about his grandparents, Ruth and Boaz; his father Jesse; his time as a shepherd; his anointment by Samuel; his service as Saul's musician; his encounter with Goliath; his promotion as commander of Saul's army; his friendship with Jonathan; Saul's attempts on his life; his alliance with the king of Moab; his association with the Philistine king of Gath; his raids with his band of six hundred men; his battle with the Amalekites; and his appointment as the king of Judah.

Why was David telling God about matters that God already knew? What was his real intent in addressing God this way? Something had struck a nerve in David, and he needed assurance. The only one who could give it to him, and perhaps correct or absolve him, was God.

Second Samuel 16:5–8 describes one of David's more challenging encounters.

As King David approached Bahurim, a man from the same clan as Saul's family came out from there. His name was Shimei, son of Gera, and he cursed as he came out. He pelted David and all the king's officials with stones, though all the troops and the special guard were on David's right and left. As he cursed, Shimei said, "Get out, get out, you murderer, you scoundrel! The Lord has repaid you for all the blood you shed in the household of Saul, in whose place you have reigned. The Lord has given the kingdom into the hands of your son Absalom. You have come to ruin because you are a murderer!"

Imagine this experience: You're feeling pretty good about yourself and your accomplishments. All of a sudden, someone comes out of nowhere and begins cursing at you, accusing and berating you in public and in the company of your supporters, friends, and family. Imagine how angry or defensive you would be. Your self-worth might suffer too. Look at the seriousness of the accusations made in the verse. Shimei didn't care about his life or reputation. He didn't care about protocol. He had something to say to the king, and he didn't mince words. Standing nearby was Abishai, one of David's military leaders. He was also David's nephew. Put yourself into the scene. Someone comes along and attacks your family member. Whose side do you take? What would you do? You would want to defend your relative, of course! Abishai, just like Peter in the Garden of Gethsemane, was ready to fight.

But look at David. Just like Jesus, he wouldn't allow any retaliation. Jesus didn't allow it because He had an assignment to carry out, and Peter's action against the high priest's servant was threatening to keep Him from it. David, on the other hand, wasn't so sure that what his accuser was saying wasn't true!

There's something about hearing the truth that makes people respond in curious ways. If it's just some random person saying something, that might be a small matter. If God says it, you might want to pay attention.

For anyone to bother to tell you the truth reveals that you're valuable to them.

Do you understand how much importance David placed on what God thought, and what God wanted? Do you see how desperately he wanted to be in the right standing with the God who loved him?

When faced with the truth, you have choices. You can try to ignore it, run away from it, hide it, or face it head on. Imagine David, a king, allowing this man to accuse him, curse at him, and attack him physically.

When David got to his destination, did he merely clean the physical dirt off himself, or did he seek to have his heart cleansed as well?

David concludes his admiration of God in verses 17 and 18 of Psalm 139: "How precious to me are your thoughts, God! How vast is the sum of them! If I were to count them, they would outnumber the grains of sand. When I awake, I am still with you."

David has no choice but to include himself in the thoughts of God. We can't help but see that there is comfort, curiosity, and even apprehension in wondering just what those thoughts are. David really wants to know.

The Lord elaborates on His own thoughts in Isaiah 55:8–9: "For my thoughts are not your thoughts, neither are your ways my ways," declares the Lord. "As the heavens are higher than the earth, so are my ways higher than your ways, and my thoughts than your thoughts."

David knew that God is both omniscient and omnipresent, yet David still drew near to Him.

David realized that God's estimation of him was much more important than what others thought. Was there any truth to what Shimei was saying? Was the cursing and stoning justified? David wanted to know. He needed to know. David knew all too well about prophecy. He was anointed while Saul was still king. He cared very much about what God thought. What if the words this man spoke were not only his opinion? What if he wasn't some raving lunatic? What if his words were actually a warning or a message from God Himself? It was important to David to know that he was in God's good graces. It should be important to us as well. Are we prepared to ask God the way David did?

Would we ignore a perfect opportunity to humiliate an enemy or, instead, seek God for His truth? David knew that God loved him. We must be confident that He loves us as well. It will greatly affect the way we approach Him.

Hebrews 4:15–16 urges believers to confide in God.

> For we do not have a high priest who cannot sympathize with our weaknesses, but One who has been tempted in all things as we are, yet without sin. Therefore let us draw near with confidence to the throne of grace, so that we may receive mercy and find grace to help in time of need.

In 1 Chronicles 28:9, David addresses his son, Solomon, on God's omniscience: "The LORD searches every heart and understands every desire and every thought."

Psalm 69:5 treats the same theme: "You, God, know my folly; my guilt is not hidden from you."

In Jeremiah 17:10, God speaks of his own omniscience: "I the LORD search the heart and examine the mind, to reward each person according to their conduct, according to what their deeds deserve."

We know that sinful deeds deserve death, as emphasized in Romans 6:23: "For the wages of sin is death, but the free gift of God is eternal life through Christ Jesus our Lord."

Again, consider the seriousness of Christ's sacrifice. Think about some of the really bad, ungodly things that David did. Despite them all, Paul reports that God spoke well of David! This approval is also reported in Acts 13:22: "After removing Saul, he made David their king. God testified concerning him: 'I have found David son of Jesse, a man after my own heart; he will do everything I want him to do.'"

Consider the truth of your own life. In spite of what you have done or said, do you deeply love God and prefer His will over your own will? I have learned to pray, "Thy will be done, in my life as it is in heaven." In heaven there is no resistance to the will of God, and that's how I want my life to be. Now rejoice in the depth of God's love. He did not love David any more than He loves you. His plan to redeem us all is proof of that. We are loved by Him—every one of us—in spite of ourselves. We have to believe it. We have to see the value in others as well as ourselves. Don't just consider the truth! Accept the truth!

CHAPTER 14

Just Believe?

To accept blindly that something is true may seem foolish. Most people want proof. To accept information as authentic, they want the word of experts, professionals, and eyewitnesses.

All around us are signs and examples of extraordinary power. There is so much in our world that we simply cannot explain. We try, but we always return to the realization that there must be someone more brilliant, wise, creative, and perfect than mere men. Creation testifies to order, organization, intricate design, and meticulous planning.

If we look at ourselves and consider the wonder that is the human body, how can we not conclude that there must be a master creator whose mind, actions, and purposes are above anything we could ever imagine?

Are we influenced by our upbringing? Do we merely follow the patterns of our families? At what point do we stop religious activity and consider whether or not the God we have heard about is actually real?

Where did we get the mind and willingness to believe? Belief is much more than assuming that there is a God somewhere. Perhaps our childhood perception of an elderly, wise gentleman resting on the clouds still fills our dreams. That powerful being far above our heads is an image from bedtime stories. The assurance that God is more than the architect introduced to us in Genesis—a living, working, ever-present, omniscient Father to us all—is a result of ingrained faith. Have you ever asked someone, "How do you know?" and the answer was, "I just know!" with no explanation or corroboration? Who gives that kind of assurance? Is our impulse to have faith within us? Are we wired to regard something as greater than ourselves?

When we believe in God, our belief is not magical. It is certain—and not of our own intellect. In the ninth chapter of Luke's gospel, verse 18, Jesus asked a peculiar question. "Once when Jesus was praying in private and his disciples were with him, he asked them, 'Who do the crowds say I am?'"

It wasn't that Jesus was confused. He wasn't being egotistical or arrogant. He wasn't looking for applause or accolades. His disciples had several responses.

"They answering said, John the Baptist; but some say, Elias; and others say, that one of the old prophets is risen again."

They did answer Christ correctly. Then He had a follow-up question: "And He said to them, 'But who do you say that I am?'"

Only one of his disciples rose to the occasion. "And Peter answered and said, 'The Christ of God.'"

How was Peter so sure that Jesus was God's Messiah? Was it because he'd studied? Had he been paying closer attention than the others? Did he have more faith? Was there a cheat sheet around? How did he know? Was it his natural intellect?

Matthew's account gives us important details. Jesus responded, "Blessed are you, Simon Bar-Jonah, for flesh and blood has not revealed this to you, but my Father, who is in heaven!"

God Himself had revealed the identity of Jesus to Peter! Peter did not wrestle with, challenge, or reject the information! He responded immediately and boldly. He probably surprised himself! Jesus called him blessed—not because of who he was or because of anything he had done, but because he had been counted worthy to receive such awesome information!

John wrote of another interchange between Jesus and Peter. Peter was asked repeatedly by Jesus, "Do you love me?" Anyone else would have been annoyed. Once you make a declaration you believe to be true, you don't think you need to repeat it. Not only did God inform Peter of the true identity of Christ, He also instructed him on how to express his love—"Feed my lambs."

God is not difficult to find. He is everywhere—showing Himself in plain sight—giving us reason after reason not only to know who He is but to believe in Him and his Word. God has given His own testimony! How can we say that we worship and praise God and go to Him in prayer if we don't first believe that He exists?

All creation was prepared to make the way for faith, trust, and belief. We were created in His image. We have the mind of God! How, then, can we say that we don't believe in Him or that He is a figment of men's imaginations? God orchestrates events expressly to inspire our belief. God exerts energy so that we believe! But is belief an exclusive act reserved for Christians?

Read James 2:19 on faith: "You say you have faith, for you believe that there is one God. Good for you! Even the demons believe this, and they tremble in terror."

We can't merely be proud that we believe in God and stop there. We believe in traffic signals too—we even think they're wonderful, necessary tools. If we don't respect or honor them, though, we could be in big trouble! It is not enough simply to believe in God and acknowledge that He's present somewhere. Demons believe that, too! God forbid that a demon should have more reverence for God than His own children!

John 6:63–65 elaborates on the Spirit/belief synergy.

> It is the Spirit who gives life; the flesh profits nothing; the words that I have spoken to you are spirit and are life, but there are some of you who do not believe." For Jesus knew from the beginning who they were who did not believe, and who it was that would betray Him. And He was saying, "For this reason I have said to you, that no one can come to me unless it has been granted him from the Father."

The lyrics of an old song urge us to "only believe." We're encouraged that "all things are possible" if we only believe. It's a lovely song, and the sentiment to believe is understood, but we have to go a step further and thank God for giving us the wherewithal to do so. In the same manner that our mortal flesh is of no value apart from our souls, our professions of belief, religious exercise, and good works are worthless apart from the divine work and revelation of the Spirit of God.

What we believe matters! Eternal life is a result of believing in the Son. Eternal life is not merely a result of hearing the Word, but believing in the one God sent to manifest it. We can't just believe in God, we must also believe in Christ—His divine representative—as well.

CHAPTER 15

Hope and Gratitude

A sure way to evaluate an individual's spirituality is not by the size of that person's Bible, his or her record of church attendance, or how many passages of Scripture the individual can quote, but the magnitude of that person's gratitude toward God and love for others. Hope is positive assurance. When a person's actions flow from hope, it becomes increasingly easy to show others that assurance. Confidence in God elucidates love for others. Because we are connected to Christ, we can conquer the selfness that robs us of natural and spiritual unity and maturity. Hope leads to growth and growth to gratitude.

We can be purposefully, wittingly grateful. Our own attitudes and circumstances can improve if we are determined to create environments where gratitude has free reign. Imagine that—we can literally make ourselves feel better and enhance our own health just by being grateful.

We can be sincerely and deeply appreciative of the kindness we've been shown by God through other people, the mercy we have been given, or the benefits we have received each day. Before we complain or seek out something or someone to denigrate, we ought to take time—a lot of time—to be grateful. Being grateful just might make us frown less and smile more. This world could certainly use more joyful, spirit-filled people.

We can perform a good service for our hearts, minds, opinions, and dispositions if we concentrate on the blessings and benefits for which we can be grateful.

According to Dictionary.com, ***Gratitude*** can be defined as "the quality or feeling of being grateful or thankful." If we consider how faithful and attentive God has been to us, we should be the world's best experts in demonstrating gratitude. It is amazing how fiercely ungrateful, self-absorbed, and forgetful people can be. People go out of their way to be gracious, extend themselves, offer help, and show brotherly love, and some think they are owed this kindness from others. No one, however, is compelled to do anything for us. No one is compelled to be nice, generous, or concerned, but when they are, it should be a relief—and another reason to be grateful.

At times, as if we have forgotten that all we have came to us out of God's goodness, we keep score of what we have done for others. Everything we have been given, however, came from God.

James 1:17 clarifies the nature of these gifts. "Every good gift and every perfect gift is from above, and cometh down from the Father of lights, with whom, is no variableness, neither shadow of turning."

We can congratulate ourselves for the good that we do but must not minimize the efforts of others. At times we may not give appropriate credit for the contributions of people who have been present in time of need. Our benefactors may then feel as if they've done nothing good at all for us. Are we brazenly guilty of failing to credit those who unselfishly sacrifice for us and to us? Sadly, unintentionally, at times we treat God the same way. Daily He wakes us up, provides all our needs, assigns angels to us, replenishes our resources, and does so much more for us. Even so, we may turn our backs to Him with disobedience, open defiance, hauteur, ill temper, and endless complaints that all manifest our unbelief.

Declarations that no one has ever done anything for us reflect pure forgetfulness! Claims that no one has ever given us anything express the gratitude of a cold heart that has forgotten what God has provided. We should repent for forgetting God's goodness in our lives.

Luke 11:13 addresses the magnitude of God's generosity. "If ye then, being evil, know how to give good gifts unto your children: how much more shall your heavenly Father give the Holy Spirit to them that ask him?"

We can *never* surpass God when it comes to giving. Gratitude, then, should be such a huge part of our being that everyone can see it. From birth to this present day, God has always been there and will always be there until the end. How dare we exclude Him and fail to be grateful?

At times we sit back and act as if God had nothing to do with all the blessings we enjoy. We should be ashamed. Can't we see how merciful God has been toward us? It is His nature to hate sin and sinfulness, yet He extended his love toward us. Should there be any limit to our gratitude? Should we ever be without hope?

Right now there are people who would love to be in your place. There are lonely people who would love to have fellowship with others. When we have opportunities, we should affirm and encourage people. There are unlucky people who can't walk, run, or even move independently; there are hungry people who would be happy with a piece of stale bread. There are lost people who have never heard of our Savior, depressed people who can feel no hope, and grieving people who feel that they have no reason to live. There are confused people with mental illness who'd give anything for a sound mind, imprisoned people whose every movement is dictated by someone else, and homeless people who'd love even the most modest shelter or simplest form of friendship.

Here we are—neither perfect nor without issues and errors, but alive and blessed with ongoing opportunities to declare the goodness of God. This would be a good time to say, "Thank you, Lord."

It might also be a good time to express repentance to God for the times we forgot how wonderful He has been to us. He makes ways for us, puts resources and people in place to make our routines easier and better, warms us with His sunshine, refreshes us with His rain, cools us with the snow, and sustains us with the fruit trees. Such adjectives as *negative, oppressive, faithless, discouraging,* and *ungrateful* should not define or describe us. Our words and actions should be filled with hope and life because of the great God we serve and His love for us. Yes, the goodness of God causes men to repent.

Deuteronomy 30:14–16 tells us about the intimate nearness of the Word.

> The word is very near you; it is in your mouth and in your heart so you may obey it. See, I set before you today life and prosperity, death and destruction. For I command you today to love the Lord your God, to walk in obedience to him, and to keep his commands, decrees and laws; then you will live and increase, and the Lord your God will bless you in the land you are entering to possess.

Consider this: Do our words have weight? We must understand the power of our words. Do we forget that we have a choice between believing in God and listening to our own faithless words, talk that is contrary to the Word of God, the words God spoke? We will experience the fruit of our own lips, as expressed in Proverbs 18:21: "The tongue has the power of life and death, and those who love it will eat its fruit."

Do we realize how important it is to think before we speak? Over the years I have counseled many married individuals, and a recurring theme was, "If only I hadn't said that!" However, it is impossible to take back what has been said, and sometimes those words do irreparable damage. It is far better to wait before we speak and think those words through first. This will help us make peace, not its opposite. We have to be careful with our words! We are warned on this subject in James 1:19:

"Wherefore, my beloved brethren, let every man be swift to hear, slow to speak, slow to wrath."

In James 3:5–6, the apostle enlarges on the impact of loose speech.

> The tongue is a small part of the body, but it makes great boasts. Consider what a great forest is set on fire by a small spark. The tongue also is a fire—a world of evil among the parts of the body. It corrupts the whole body, sets the whole course of one's life on fire, and is itself set on fire by hell.

Do we understand that we don't have to say everything that pops into our heads? Do we know how damaging and deadly our words can be to ourselves and others? Sometimes the quickest and best way to steer clear of potentially dangerous talk is to abandon the need to be right all the time.

Gratitude inspires compassion, kindness, and mercy toward others. Gratitude doesn't repel others. If we are grateful, we are not compelled to have the last word in every disagreement.

Our demeanor should encourage others to want to hear what we have to say. Do we pay attention to the way we speak to others? Are we representatives of the Most High God grateful? Do we acknowledge how much we appreciate Christ's sacrifice on Calvary? He did the work, and it was sufficient and complete. Hebrews 7:27 reminds us: "He sacrificed for their sins once for all when he offered himself."

Gratitude to God requires decreased egotism and increased appreciation of who He is. Gratitude to God requires us to see ourselves the way He sees us—loved, saved, redeemed, accepted, freed, healed, whole, and delivered. Gratitude and doubt cannot occupy the same space.

Gratitude is and should be our reply to the wonderful hope we have in Jesus Christ. We should be the last people to be proudly mean-spirited, angry, tight-fisted, stubborn, cruel, critical, rigid, and unloving. We are the recipients of the goodness, mercy, grace, and blessings of God.

Psalm 138:1–8 is all about David's gratitude. There is no way we can read it and remain in any hopeless or ungrateful state.

> I will praise you, Lord, with all my heart; before the "gods" I will sing your praise. I will bow down toward your holy temple and will praise your name for your unfailing love and your faithfulness, for you have so exalted your solemn decree that it surpasses your fame. When I called, you answered me; you greatly emboldened me. May all the kings of the earth praise you, Lord, when they hear what you have decreed. May they sing of the ways of the Lord, for the glory of the Lord is great. Though the Lord is exalted, he looks kindly on the lowly; though lofty, he sees them from afar. Though I walk in the midst of trouble, you preserve my life. You stretch out your hand against the anger of my foes; with your right hand you save me. The Lord will vindicate me; your love, Lord, endures forever—do not abandon the works of your hands.

David could say those words because he believed them in his heart! He could address God with such familiarity because he had been delivered so many times by God. In fact, speaking of himself in Psalm 34:6, David wrote, "This poor man called, and the LORD heard him; he saved him out of all his troubles." David was an anointed king on the run for his life. He saw himself as a poor man even though God had anointed him as king. We might see ourselves one way, but is our way the one God sees when He looks at us? He saved us for a reason and purpose. There is more in you than what you see. David glorified God and was thankful! How about you? What will you do? How can we see the hand of God in our lives so many times and still deny ourselves the joy of glorifying God, who has brought us through so many trials and tests? Truth and love are built upon hope, and obviously David's hope was in the Lord.

Luke 6:45 describes the link between our inner conditions and our outward expressions: "A good man brings good things out of the good stored up in his heart, and an evil man brings evil things out of the evil stored up in his heart. For the mouth speaks what the heart is full of."

The feeling in the human heart will come out of the mouth. An angry heart yields angry speech. A wounded heart produces wounded speech. A grateful heart articulates grateful speech. A hopeful heart manifests itself in hopeful speech.

God remembers us, comforts us, and encourages us to draw near to Him. Do we draw near, or do we decide that our own truth or reality is more important? God does not act on our timetable; He is faithful all the time, and we can believe Him.

Second Peter 3:8 reminds us of God's divine overview of time: "But do not forget this one thing, dear friends: With the Lord a day is like a thousand years, and a thousand years are like a day."

God constantly covers and protects us. I cannot say that enough. Misunderstanding of God and His word and unbelief regarding God's identity, works, and promises render all that we do useless. We may as well put away our books, paper, and pens. If we come away with nothing else, we have to know how important it is to believe and trust God and His Word wholeheartedly. It will radically change our words and actions. It will change our minds and hearts. It will affect how we interact with and treat others. It will revolutionize how we look at our own lives, purposes, gifts, and talents. It will alter how we spend our time and our choices of mentors and prayer partners.

Belief will inspire us to be more honest, more authentic, and less pretentious. It will affect our outlook as we walk by faith each day and help us see the goodness and beauty in life. It will soften our hearts. If we have hope, we have faith. If we have faith, we can please God, as explained in Hebrews 11:6: "And without faith it is impossible to please God, because anyone who comes to him must believe that he exists and that he rewards those who earnestly seek him."

When we seek to please God, our every action will be dedicated to His glory. We will be able to endure even the most difficult, uncomfortable circumstances and people and still let our lights shine. Let gratefulness and a hopeful spirit so infuse you that others will be encouraged and drawn to God because of you.

Be grateful. Have hope. Demonstrate it daily.

Romans 8:28 captures the divine intention: "And we know that in all things God works for the good of those who love him, who have been called according to his purpose."

Psalm 5:11 describes the joy that comes with knowledge of that intention: "But let all who take refuge in you be glad; let them ever sing for joy. Spread your protection over them that those who love your name, may rejoice in you."

Be grateful. Have hope. Demonstrate it daily, as expressed in 2 Corinthians 1:20: "For no matter how many promises God has made, they are 'Yes' in Christ. And so through him the 'Amen' is spoken by us to the glory of God."

The Message Bible translates the passage as follows.

> Whatever God has promised gets stamped with the Yes of Jesus. In him, this is what we preach and pray, the great Amen, God's "Yes" and our "Yes" together, gloriously evident. God affirms us, making us a sure thing in Christ, putting his Yes within us. By his Spirit he has stamped us with his eternal pledge—a sure beginning of what he is destined to complete.

Second Thessalonians 2:16–17 is an apt text for a conclusion. Be grateful. This life, even with its challenges, can be so wonderful and full of possibilities if we only stay focused on our great and loving God—"May our Lord Jesus Christ himself and God our Father, who loved us and by his grace gave us eternal encouragement and good hope, encourage your hearts and strengthen you in every good deed and word."

It truly does not matter where you came from or how many times you have been let down or have fallen. Where you are going does matter. Your destiny is tied up in your faith in God! Don't just believe that there is a God; believe and live by His words. Receive His mercy today. After we accept Jesus by faith into our hearts, we move from mercy to grace. As we learn of God and walk by God's Word, we grow in grace, and we manifest His glory in earthly life.

And we know that every word and every deed we do in this life will be judged by God at the end. No good or bad deed will go unnoticed or unjudged by God. The goal is not to have more good deeds than bad, but to allow the love of God to enter our hearts by faith. The chief purpose of humanity is to glorify God! Glorification of God starts with receiving His mercy, then growing in His grace, and finally reflecting His glory!

Decide to live wittingly every day.

ABOUT THE AUTHOR

Bishop Edward Barnett is the founder and pastor of Greater Grace Family Ministries Church. Its foundation was in 1991, when he returned from a trip to Africa. There the Lord gave him the name and mission for the church.

Bishop Barnett was born in Washington, DC and educated in the public schools there. In the early 1980s, he helped the late Rev. Conrad Brooks establish the Christian Praise Church in Washington, DC, serving in evangelism and the men's ministry, and was selected as deacon. He was called into the ministry in 1982 and ordained in 1986. He served his pastor until his calling to the pastorate was evident in 1990.

He started Greater Grace Family Ministries Church with the support of his loving wife of twenty-nine years, First Lady Adrienne H. Barnett, his sons, and three other families. After twenty-four years, the ministry is still flowing in the anointing of the Holy Spirit; bonds are loosed, the oppressed are set free, curses are broken, spiritual maturity is evident in believers, and the spiritual leadership is focused and connected to the divine godhead to carry out divine purpose.

Bishop Barnett has had many souls saved by God while training candidates for the ministry through Greater Grace Family Ministries Church. Some went on to work elsewhere in the kingdom of God as deacons, ministers, pastors, and evangelists.

Bishop Barnett has earned a BA in business management, an advanced professional certification in anger management, and MA degrees in theology and professional counseling. He was ordained as a bishop by the College of Bishops on January 19, 2013. He received a PhD in Humanities January 2014.

He still enjoys watching the power of God move in the marketplaces of the world. Currently he is the director of residential services for a nonprofit that serves the mentally ill in Washington, DC. He oversees two supportive residential facilities, a crisis home, and a supported independent living program housing over fifty mental health consumers. He has substance abuse counseling certification through Catholic Charities, an accredited substance abuse program. His oversight of staff is invaluable and productive, his trainings are thoroughly informative, yet he remains humble and simple.

Bishop Barnett has preached and ministered throughout the Washington, DC metropolitan area and Pennsylvania, Ohio, and Virginia. In 1991 he traveled to northeast Africa on a missionary journey. He spent many hours counseling, preaching, and teaching the Word of God in Nairobi, Kenya, and in Sudan, Uganda, and the Rift Valley area. While he was in Mombasa, more than a thousand people gave their lives to Christ in a crusade. In March 2014 he returned to Kenya and also visited Katamega, Kisimu, Nairobi, and Uganda. He conducted pastoral and leadership training throughout those regions. He oversees many churches in western Kenya.

From the beginning onward, God has drawn many to be trained in leadership and service for God, with a kingdom-building mindset out in the world.

In 2017 The entire City Council of Washington DC honored Dr Barnett with "Bishop Dr. Edward Barnett Recognition Resolution of 2017"

In 2019 Dr. Edward Barnett was appointed an "Ambassador of Peace" by UPF/NGO connected to United Nations.

Bishop Barnett always encourages "Be excited by the challenges, create opportunities, expect the best"

Council of the District of Columbia

Resolution

COUNCILMEMBER T. WHITE

COUNCILMEMBER ALLEN	COUNCILMEMBER BONDS	COUNCILMEMBER CHEH
COUNCILMEMBER EVANS	COUNCILMEMBER GRAY	COUNCILMEMBER GROSSO
COUNCILMEMBER McDUFFIE	CHAIRMAN MENDELSON	COUNCILMEMBER NADEAU
COUNCILMEMBER SILVERMAN	COUNCILMEMBER TODD	COUNCILMEMBER R. WHITE

BISHOP DR. EDWARD BARNETT RECOGNITION RESOLUTION OF 2017

WHEREAS, BISHOP DR. EDWARD BARNETT IS THE FOUNDER OF GREATER GRACE FAMILY MINISTRIES AND HAS SERVED FOR TWENTY-SIX YEARS;

WHEREAS, BISHOP DR. EDWARD BARNETT HAS TRAVELED INTERNATIONALLY AS A PREACHER. HE HAS ALSO TAUGHT PASTORS IN KENYA, AFRICA;

WHEREAS, BISHOP DR. EDWARD BARNETT IS A FATHER OF THREE AND HAS BEEN MARRIED FOR THIRTY-ONE YEARS;

WHEREAS, BISHOP DR. EDWARD BARNETT HAS EARNED TWO PHDS, TWO MASTERS DEGREES, AND TWO ADVANCED STUDIES DEGREES;

WHEREAS, BISHOP DR. EDWARD BARNETT HAS SERVED AS A DIRECTOR IN MENTAL HEALTH ORGANIZATIONS IN WASHINGTON DC FOR TWENTY-NINE YEARS;

WHEREAS, BISHOP DR. EDWARD BARNETT HAS ALSO BEEN A RADIO PRODUCER AND HOST FOR THREE YEARS AT WEACT RADIO AND WBGR;

WHEREAS, BISHOP DR. EDWARD BARNETT WAS ELEVATED TO BISHOP IN 2013;

WHEREAS, HE IS THE AUTHOR OF "LIVING WITTINGLY" AND IS IN THE PROCESS OF WRITING TWO OTHER BOOKS, "THREATS TO MARRIAGE" AND MENTAL HEALTH IN THE CHURCH";

WHEREAS, BISHOP DR. EDWARD BARNETT WAS RECENTLY INTERVIEWED ON CHRISTIAN TV IN ATLANTA GEORGIA; AND

RESOLVED, BY THE COUNCIL OF THE DISTRICT OF COLUMBIA, THAT THIS RESOLUTION MAY BE CITED AS THE "BISHOP DR. EDWARD BARNETT RECOGNITION RESOLUTION OF 2017".

SEC. 2. THE COUNCIL OF THE DISTRICT OF COLUMBIA RECOGNIZES BISHOP DR. EDWARD BARNETT ON THE OCCASION OF HIS TWENTY-SIXTH CHURCH ANNIVERSARY.

This resolution shall take effect immediately.

_____
CHAIRMAN OF THE COUNCIL

I hereby Certify that this Resolution is true and adopted as stated herein.

Resolution Number   CER 22-192

Date   October 3, 2017

_____
SECRETARY TO THE COUNCIL

Dr. Barnett was Recognized by the entire Washington DC City Council for his service in 2017, for his work in the community and the field of Mental Health.

Contact information

Bishop Dr. Edward Barnett

www.Livingwittingly@gmail.com or www.ggfm1@msn.com

web site: www.greatergracefamilyministries.org

Mailing address:

Bishop Dr. Edward Barnett

P. O. Box 568

Upper Marlboro, MD 20773

CPSIA information can be obtained
at www.ICGtesting.com
Printed in the USA
BVHW041922230322
632288BV00020B/264